Hot Metal Cold Beer

Farewell the Fourth Estate

Paul Campbell

Hot Metal, Cold Beer
Paul Campbell

© 2024 Oxford eBooks Ltd.

www.oxford-ebooks.com

The right of the author to be identified as the author of this work
has been asserted in accordance with the
Copyright, Designs and Patents Act 1988.

All rights reserved.
No part of this publication may be reproduced, stored in a retrieval system, or
transmitted, in any form or by any means, electronic, mechanical, photocopying,
recording or otherwise, without the prior permission of the copyright owners.

ISBN 978-1-910779-44-6

Oxford eBooks

"'A lie gets halfway around the world before the truth gets its pants on.' In our age, a lie can get a thousand times around the world before the truth gets its pants on."

Jim Mattis, on Winston Churchill.

PRELUDE

WHAT HAS HAPPENED to my craft, the Fourth Estate that I and my peers have made our lifelong vocation?

At a time when retirement and pleasant reminiscence beckons, pride in personal achievements in newspapers, wire services, magazines, radio and television, as well as a number of book titles, in a dozen countries, has been tempered by despair for the future.

I blame the Internet, but I also shudder at the product of so-called technical institute journalism courses and the television x-factor preoccupation valued over good training, experience and ability. In media today, apart from obvious right or left wing bias, there is a minefield of mistakes ranging from punctuation to fantasy.

We dinosaurs of the business always said that the facts should never stand in the way of a good story, a cliché hopefully confined to an after work beer. Today it has become reality. What is printed today is tomorrow's fish and chip paper but that doesn't mean it should not be reported accurately. There is an endless list of inept headline writing usually applied to non-news, that would have hit the bust-spike on any outlet I ever worked for. 'Woman Wet Herself While Trapped in Carpark Queue' was a heading in the online version of a self-declared 'best journalism' metropolitan daily.

I am aware it is all down to readership competition

in a digital media saturated world. But the carnage is compounded as newspaper sub-editing, the core character base for any newspaper, is today farmed out to a central subbery – a gaggle of editorial battery hens. Instead of imparting the genus of a newspaper to his readers, the sub-editor of today processes stories for any number of publications with nary a thought for location, local custom, idiom or usage, or even an essential questioning of fact.

News bosses boast also of 'national centres of expertise'; to carry out sub-editing, layout and production for all news, features, and business pages for a dozen different publications. These facilities are likely to be offshore and bereft of local knowledge. Quality is the casualty.

But we are not just faced with a coronary occlusion in the newspaper editing world. Reporters are no longer needed either. On news websites around the globe publications solicit with all the panache of a street-corner hooker. "Are you in the flooded area? Send us your story and pictures" they plead. "Do you know anything about the shooting? Contact us!"

Technology has created an instant world-wide reporting and photographic staff of inept millions, all of them unchecked. Everyone has the privilege of transmission. So much so that printed newspapers have relied on social media to the extent of including links to, for instance X, as a source for particular detail.

With cell phones that photograph stills and video, and have Internet connection, television news is following this decline. The remote discipline discovered in the Covid pandemic has now been accepted as a cheap alternative to physical contact in interviews. Standards of accuracy and presentation of facts once instilled into every journalist before exiting the ranks of a three-to-four-year training cadetship, are disappearing.

The media has lost its way. It is there to report events, not to create them. And audiences are perceptive. Trust in the Fourth Estate is diminishing the world over. Lessons learned as a cadet journalist in a devastating roar across the newsroom from the Chief Sub-editor have also been thrown out the window. To exacerbate the mess the craft is in today, about 16,000 words of the English language have succumbed to pressures of the internet age and lost hyphens in the Shorter Oxford English Dictionary.

Bumble-bee is now bumblebee, ice-cream is icecream and pot-belly is pot belly. And sub-editor has become – but of course, you've got it. The hyphen has fallen under the onslaught of the cell phone text message and the Internet with its informal shorthand.

"People are not confident about using hyphens any more, they are not really sure what they are for," says the dictionary editor.

Punctuation is seen as messy looking and old-fashioned and not only that, the situation will not improve with an education system that allows *txt spk* abbreviations in education examinations. But even more messy are modern ivory tower linguists who push a theory that fullstops, or full-stops? are going to 'upset' young people brought up on *txt msg* because they might see the punctuation as a 'curt and passive aggression – Bloody hell!

Don't get me started though on AI and its bleak creative future, It all signals an epitaph for the Fourth Estate, a craft I chose with great excitement in 1963 and that has sustained my life across the world in a dozen countries for six decades. But let's start that story covering some of the better times in my industry and I'll come back to the miserable stuff at the end of my account.

CHAPTER ONE

AT MIDNIGHT ON a Friday, sometime in March 1963, the giant Uniman rotary press rumbled the foundations deep in the belly of *The Daily News* building and the hot metal linotype machines on the production floor rattled into silence. The solidified detritus of molten lead was being swept up from the composing shop floor for re-melting into tomorrow's news.

The Taranaki, New Zealand, provincial paper had 'gone to bed' and with a couple of other late shift reporters I headed to supper at Ping's Piecart near the darkened New Plymouth public library, a hamburger to devour and a hopeful chat with Ping's attractive daughter and waitress Daisy, before the short drive home to sleep. Home for me was in the suburban house I shared with my parents and sisters, paying board to Mum in the then currency of 30 shillings from my princely weekly wage of five guineas – perhaps worth $50 today.

I had landed this job, which proved to be a life changing and adventurous career choice pretty much by accident. At the age of 16 I was considered at skeletal adulthood so major orthopaedic surgery did away with childhood metal calliper support, stabilising the bones of my right ankle with my lower leg wasted of muscle in the 1948 poliomyelitis pandemic.

The surgical intervention was successful in achieving an internal bone stability but continued a lifelong limp with a right leg shorter than my left and partially corrected by a built-up shoe. Post surgery I was many months in a plaster cast but a journalism career beckoned after scholastic success in the subject of English comprehension, engendered no doubt by intensive reading in convalescent bouts and access to my schoolmaster grandfather's extensive library. *Arthur Mee's Children's Encyclopaedia* was also a youthful bible from my mother.

In point of fact, my father had a quiet beer in a pub frequented by local newspaper identities and set up a contact that he said I should follow up on. I took his opening and stepped through a doorway to my future.

Accepted after a stern interview with *The Daily News* Editor, John Fullerton, my leg in a walking plaster 'boot', my career training began in the proof-reading room at 6pm each day, correcting the punctuation of livestock prices at cattle sales, grammar and spelling in news and feature stories for the next edition before they were set in stone by the old hot metal process.

My tutelage began seated comfortably under the hooded fluorescent lights over the desk, supervised by the redoubtable Chief Reader, Peggy Herdson and her three staff. I learned the skills of communicating copy changes that we marked in a shorthand code on galley proofs, inked from the hot metal type set in iron page forms that would make their way through the printing process. Out on the production floor on the first level of the Daily News building in the downtown area, the lines of leaden amalgam typesetting spilled in segments from clanking linotype machines. Operators at clicking and mysterious built-in keyboards transformed molten metal from internal cauldrons into cooled 'slugs' of words. The whole process produced a background roar and metallic aura that I can still hear and smell, decades later, in my sleep. Compositors transferred the slugs into columns that made up stories that were collectively locked into page forms. Before this though, a galley-proof was inked from the metal type to arrived on a spring-loaded 'rapid wire' suspended from the ceiling through a portal between the production floor and the proofreading room. Corrections were marked in pencil and sent back to the process.

So one galley arriving might be the heading, or 'head' with the actual story known as the 'tail' for 'tale' arriving separately. This system of course had its pitfalls and I was regaled with stories about when a compositing worker found a dead mouse. What better opportunity to use the rapid wire system to send 'head, and then 'tail follows' My fellow readers swore it had happened but I reckon it was a job anecdote as I was to hear of many similar newspaper legends in the years to come. If it had happened it would only have been once because, funnily enough Mrs Herdson would have not been at all amused.

One night a week, I was able to start my shift two hours late. Part of my official employment time involved learning shorthand for note-taking. Evening classes in the Pitmans skill were held at a local college where I was the lone male. A dozen attractive secretarial-bound young ladies made up the rest of the class. Well, I certainly made sure I was in diligent attendance and managed to learn some, but it was not the best place for a young bloke to concentrate on his penmanship.

Fortunately, some eight months of proofreading, while instilling a certain discipline in my learning the ropes, ended with a new first step.

A vacancy had opened in the newsroom when the cadet ahead of me was transferred out to one of two line offices operating in the province. He was Trevor Hawkins and a friendship formed then has lasted across six decades and continues as I write this.

Now freed from my walking plaster I was mobile and raring to go and get into print. A week's wages disappeared on a brand new portable Imperial Good Companion typewriter in a fibreglass carrying case which, clad in regulation collar and tie and a new sports coat, I proudly placed on my allocated desk space among reporters at one end of the large newsroom. At the other, the Chief Sub-Editor Bill Morrison oversaw his team of subs at a long table that backed into the wall of my former home in the proof reading enclave. The air reeked of tobacco smoke and the sound of clacking of typewriter keys, ringing telephones, murmured conversation into them and shouted messages across the space as needed. It was heady front page movie stuff but I was soon brought down to earth.

I began with the intricacies of the weather map that I laboriously traced with a nib in black India ink from a series of teleprinter number combinations onto graph paper. This was then transferred into an engraved half-tone plate depiction which was in turn locked into a page form. Black and white was the order of the day with colour rendition then far in the future Photographs were also half-tones produced on an auto gravure machine in the photographic department, den of the staff photographers who specialised in their profession.

Another major learning curve as a cadet was 'the round'. We had our agriculture or farming reporter, expected to quote the latest meat and wool prices in pastoral New Zealand at the drop of a pen. There was the police roundsman expected to know the ins and outs of crime statistics and the doings of constabulary and detectives, the business page financial expert, the city roundsman who had the ear of the mayor and council, and so on.

This too was a time when the training of journalists was highly regimented. At the time in New Zealand almost every large town and some smaller, had their own newspaper titles requiring a large national staffing pool. New Plymouth had two papers with the afternoon *Taranaki Herald* becoming our opposition. This of course made for competition and scoring a beat, a scoop, was a great incentive to strive. But training was the operative word and it was a long haul for staff in those days.

A cadet could look forward to four years of toil, rising in annual salary grades from one through four, before becoming a Junior five through six years to General Reporter, years seven through nine. Then on approval, the magic accolade of Senior Reporter would apply before the super-rank of Senior Special, by which time one would expect to be at executive level at least a Deputy Chief Reporter. It was a daunting ladder, but one I was to find could be surmounted in a much speedier timeframe. I was to realise that in some part due a regimented training regime, Kiwi journalists earned respect in newsrooms around the planet.

For the moment though I was now a second year cadet, by virtue of my proof reading experience and had my first news round. The Shipping Reporter! This involved keeping the newspaper's thumb on what ships were due in Port Taranaki at the southern end of town, what ships were loading or discharging cargo, and when they would sail and to where. This was a time when coastal shipping was New Zealand's major inward and outward conduit for goods and services, preceding the rise of highly mechanised road transport. Rail was also important for onward land transfer.

The shipping column appeared daily and pretty much relied on a call to the harbour master's office from where occasionally an actual news story emerged. One such was a tip that a Holm Shipping Company freighter had weathered a major storm in passage on the west coast on her way in.

Off I went on the office motor scooter to interview the captain about the adventure with photographer Peter McCabe to do the honours. Well, we got the picture and story, but I learned a great lesson in so doing. The skipper was a Norwegian old sea dog with a large liquor cabinet and I at least was a little too enthusiastic in accepting his hospitality in order to elicit some good quotes of storms at sea, master's derring do and intrepid crew's bravery and such.

From memory, McCabe drove the office motor scooter back to the paper, I assume I was clinging on the pillion. After some office administered hot coffee and slow typing the story appeared and I was blooded in the craft, faking nonchalance but walking on air as my family read my first real news report in the paper next morning.

Stories flowed over the next 18 months as I covered local events and activities. There were surf carnivals, agricultural shows, house and bush fires, various motor accidents, provincial council meetings and just odd stories gleaned from an office chore that fell to whoever was on hand at the time. Around five in the evening, a reporter would ring half a dozen hotels in neighbouring towns, to ask "Is anyone interesting in the pub, anything of interest in town?"

On one of my calls I was told a local Member of Parliament was in-house and I was emboldened to ask if I could speak to him as a news check. The hotel receptionist went to ask and came back to report she didn't really think so. "He is in the house bar and... well, he can't really come to the phone just now. At least I think that's the polite way of telling you." I moved on to the next call. Next day that worthy MP resigned and sparked a by-election making national news. It would not be the only 'near miss' in my experience.

However, there were landmark events too and I will always remember an assignment to cover the arrival of an aerial top dressing plane at New Plymouth airport. It was a good story opportunity and result but it also earned me a bollocking from the Chief

Reporter (aka God) for actually getting my interview with the pilot from the vacant co-pilot's seat a few hundred feet or so and at 150 miles an hour over the rolling Taranaki farming country below being treated with aerial fertiliser.

"You are not insured for stunts like that Campbell. It's a no no." I did have a thought for the number 8 wire holding the wartime relic Lockheed Hudson's rattling door closed, but did not elaborate on this and Dennis Garcia's quiet smile eased the rebuke somewhat.

A fledgling cadet reporter's life back in the middle of last century was very mundane and included the task of seeking obituary material in the case of a death. The worst such assignment was in the case of a tragic accident, when I had to knock on the door of a grieving family to ask as diplomatically as possible for details and a photo. I was always amazed though at the usual calm acceptance of my newspaper job, the cup of tea offered, and a willingness to talk about the deceased. Occasionally though there was an angry response, probably shock driven.

One adventure still engenders night terrors when it spills from my memory bank. I accompanied the Taranaki Speleological Society, a caving enthusiast group, on a weekend visit to a remote section of the Awakino Gorge, 90 miles north of town. After overnighting at a farm shearer's quarters and a tractor-trailer journey into some back country we entered a cave halfway up a high bush-clad hill and proceeded down to the depths. At the lowest point in the bowels of the earth, we were forced to crawl on hands and knees through a long low narrow passage hewn by a stream, known to my guides as 'a squeeze'. The water was most fortunately shallow at the time. I concentrated on the rear of a young lady caver in front of me in the beam of my helmet lantern, so managed to suppress a seriously rising panic with impure thoughts. We thankfully emerged into a wider cavern adorned with stalagmites and 'tites, and then finally, thank the gods, into the open air a mile on the other side of the hill. The trip earned me accolades for the feature story that followed but I have never, ever, ventured underground since for any reason whatsoever.

In today's media regime I would have had a by-line. Back then, it was simply 'by a Staff Reporter'. I did note to my mates at the time that I was probably one of very few people to have driven on the surface, flown above in my top-dressing ride-along and travelled deep underground, all in the Awakino Gorge.

After almost two years that rite of adult passage, the overseas adventure or 'The Big OE' in the vernacular, began to dominate conversation with some of my peers in the game, usually over a break at the local coffee bar downtown. In fact on a quiet news day, Garcia often suggested we 'get out of the office and look around'. Coffee and a yarn seemed a good idea. At some of these gatherings an urge to travel and see the world emerged, perhaps sparked by the fact we lived in an isolated country at the bottom of the globe. Heading off to see a world we could only taste in the foreign cable pages would require planning and preparation for an extended expedition.

Getting to Britain, our target in those days, was a major undertaking.

As it transpired, minimal funds meant four of us plumped to start our odyssey in Australia, and then work our way onwards. Fruit picking appeared a lucrative source of income and it wasn't long before plans were made and four young journalists, myself, Trevor Hawkins, Bob Adlam and Mike O'Neil from the *Taranaki Herald* took the overnight train journey to Auckland, farewelled by a small crowd of family and well-wishers. After another night at the now extinct Great Northern Hotel in Auckland, we bussed to the airport that was then part of a Royal New Zealand Air Force base in West Auckland. There we boarded what was the last De Havilland Comet jet service out of the country, landing some three hours later in Sydney Australia.

CHAPTER TWO

It was a false start to an eventual OE, that for me would consume decades and a dozen or so countries, but back then I think we had our sights set simply and temporarily on lucrative employment in Australia to pay for our onward world journey. This so-called 'plan' involved applying for 'high commission' sales positions which turned out to be flogging Colliers Encyclopedias door to door in some low-rent Sydney suburbs. I remember we opted for the job because having a passport was 'a work requirement', suggesting to us at the time there was a prospect of free job travel. That lasted one door-knocking night for us. Then it was off on the train to Brisbane and another 'money-saving' opportunity picking fruit at highly paid rates with accommodation thrown in. It became a day in Queensland eating the luxury of cheap prawns, a night at the noisy YMCA hostel and finding the jobs were in the middle of nowhere with conditions and wages far from those advertised.

With limited funds, Hawkins and I decided to retreat to New Zealand and find jobs in a more familiar Auckland to replenish our coffers.

We flew home pretty broke and curled up under a bushy tree in Auckland's central Albert Park for some shuteye pillowed on our bags before an early morning bus ride down country and home, But those were the days of police constables on 'the beat' rather than patrol cars and we were swiftly located in torchlight.

After explanations we were directed to the city bus terminal to wait on bloody hard wooden benches for our dawn transport.

But a few weeks on with the last of some bank savings we were back in Auckland and I was hired by NZ Truth which back then in late 1965 was a very successful gutter press rag that sold well in the austere company of the wholesome traditional press.

One of my main roles was reporting the more salacious details of court cases and as part of that round, record the divorce court decisions with ever an eye for the identity of a co-respondent, the third member of an adultery triangle. It was also a step up the grading ladder as a junior reporter two years ahead of my *Daily News* prospects. As always, there was the chance to earn extra money with the odd 'rat' – writing for another publication under an assumed by-line or just anonymously. Another colleague and subsequent lifelong friend until he died in Indonesia was *Taranaki Herald* reporter, John McBeth. He went on in later years to become a prominent correspondent in Asia, where our paths often crossed. He had a column in the *Herald's* evening Saturday sports edition and I attended a concert in Auckland Town Hall, and supplied John with a review. In *'Go, Go, Go- the Column with the Rhythm of Youth'* he headlined 'P.J. Proby Splits His Jeans in Auckland'

It was at Truth that I had my one and only brush with things legal after I made a trip home by car to New Plymouth. Before departing for Australia I had sold my distinctive Ford Pilot car to a man I knew to be a foreman with the local Clifton County Council.

On the main road near New Plymouth there were road works and I spotted my old car and its new owner laboriously writing down numbers of vehicles deemed driving too fast over new seal. One of my last *Daily News* stories had been about the council cutting its contribution to a new airport to save money and as this was a Sunday, I wrote a story for Truth about a waste of ratepayers money employing a man at time-and-a-half to monitor traffic. This resulted in a formal letter threatening legal action for 'libelling the council'. The road in question was in fact administered by the government National Roads Board. Oh Dear! The editor rather ominously asked me to explain myself.

I rang my Dad to check that the same bloke did have my car and he made a few discreet inquiries. The result was that my car buyer had access to the keys to council yards. He had been contracting council machinery out to the roads board and pocketing the proceeds. I was quickly off the hook from a very embarrassed council.

But the urge for travel was still strong and both Hawkins and I saved our pay living in a cheap flat conversion of an old suburban villa and soon resumed the venture we'd set out upon, booking passage back to Sydney on the *SS Aurelia*, an Italian conversion of a wartime German ship given to Canada as a spoil of war that some referred to as once being Herman Goering's private yacht. We were looked after by a pleasant Greek steward at our shared six berth steerage cabin and three or four days later were back across the Tasman.

This time I was more pragmatic and decided to stick to my knitting. I soon landed a job on the staff of *The Canberra Times* in the Australian Capital Territory. The ACT was the home of the Federal Parliament, major public services and modern and up-to-date everything. I walked into the *Times* office on a cold canvas, but after an interview with the Chief of Staff Neville Braidwood, I was told there was not a vacancy "just now but I will let you know if something comes up." I knew there were a dozen out of town newspaper bureaus at parliament, so wasn't yet too disappointed. But I was a few paces along the footpath in Mort Street, Braddon when Braidwood called me back to the door. "I've just had a bloke resign. Can you start tomorrow?"

I was soon a mid-graded general reporter, police roundsman, aviation correspondent and daily assignment man earning a good salary on this esteemed newspaper and with it the door opened to my career proper. I soon shared a suburban house with other colleagues who included Trevor Hawkins after he also arrived in town to fill a job I knew was coming up on the *Times*. Stories we produced were carbon copied to out of town news bureaus and Trev's good writing was spotted and he was soon poached by the *Melbourne Sun* bureau in the federal parliamentary press gallery.

Canberra was a young and vibrant city that threw up a kaleidoscope of life. My police round, with evening visits in an office-labelled Volkswagen sedan to the 'cop-shop' and the ambulance base on the shores of the artificially created Lake Burley Griffin threw up my first major story on the worst traffic accident I have ever covered.

A cup of tea with the ambo-crew turned into a screaming siren chase out to the highway near the New South Wales border town of Queanbeyan. Two crowded families in Aussie-built Holden station wagons had collided head-on near the HMAS Harman naval communications base.

With multiple casualties and me in the front line with the relief effort, suffice to say when I had filed my copy on multiple dead and injured at the end of the night, I found myself with several beers in the house bar of the Canberra Rex hotel, a popular media late night watering hole.

The highway crash and carnage was a baptism of fire of sorts and there followed numerous stories of misfortune, a nasty child murder, police malfeasance and others of major events politically. In the many facets life throws up for the media I had a lovely interview with Sir Edmund Hillary, in town for some funding work for his treasured Nepalese in the foothills of his conquered Mt. Everest.

Occasionally on a very quiet news day we might be assigned to the Australian National War Memorial Museum to do a vox-pops on visitor reaction. I have to admit that at least some of the "what a wonderful visit we are having to your lovely city" quotes attributed to 'Jean from Toowoomba' were written over a beer in the Jungle Bar at the Civic Hotel a block from the *Times* office. But it was considered harmless stuff. What else would they say?

Notable on the work front was the disappearance

one fine day of a Malaysian diplomat. It was June 11th 1966 when Malaysian High Commissioner Tun Lim Yew Hock vanished from the cocktail circuit sparking a national police alert. Rumours abounded, and I had a feeling that because of diplomatic immunity, the normal police sources might not be the best at this time. So in my office Volkswagen, I set off and parked in a 'stake out' in sight of the high commission doors. This was a few days after the disappearance and as luck would have it, I spotted an official looking car arrive and disgorge several figures. I duly approached the residence, but was greeted by a guard shaking an emphatic head and closing the doors. In fact the visitor was an emissary from Tunku Abdul Rahman, Malaysia's Prime Minister, intent on solving the mystery. I finally recorded the Tun's return after ten days awol, which was the stuff of a novel. It appeared he had flown off to Sydney under an assumed name and was in fact a frequent visitor to Sydney's version of a red-light district, King's Cross. This was narrowed down to the Paradise Club, and top flight and expensive stripper, Sandra Nelson. The Tun was allegedly brought home by what the embassy insisted was "a good samaritan who looked after him after he had simply fallen ill." There was not much concrete detail forthcoming – diplomatic immunity again. But the playful envoy was soon back in his own country, replaced surely by someone less adventurous.

CHAPTER THREE

AT THE END of 1966, a diplomatic contact let me know the South African Embassy was looking for a journalist to assist in publishing a magazine. I perked up my ears possibly because I a had a well established romantic view of the dark continent from reading Wilbur Smith's novels. But I confess to also knowing from my aviation reporting that South African Airways was due to start a Boeing 707 route between Johannesburg and Sydney. That and the opportunity to look into the rarified air of the diplomatic belt prompted my interview and acceptance of the job. I did a crash course with some senior colleagues on magazine production and was soon elevated to the exalted rank of an Assistant Information Attache.

True to form, in March 1967 I was included as a familiarisation duty on the return inaugural flight from Australia to South Africa. That was an eye-opener. Flying via Perth and Mauritius to Johannesburg's Jan Smuts airport, the passengers consisted mainly of travel agents from whom the airline was bent on getting favourable reviews and generated sales, a smattering of trade people and the Mayor of Sydney and his daughter. Also aboard was an Australian Broadcasting Commission television reporter and cameraman and finding kindred spirits saw me accompany them on their assignments across South Africa while the travel agents did the social rounds. Starting with a first night at the very grand

Edward Hotel in Durban and a large cooked breakfast that would have fed a platoon I learned this was all complimentary. "You don't put your hand in your pocket man," was a tour minder's instruction. We were surely guests of the government of which he was certainly an official.

Travelling with the ABC team meant I saw the country up close with the guys filming in Cape Town, Johannesburg and the Kruger National Park. In Cape Town we were escorted by two very big white policemen and we appreciated them because apart from providing us with a motorcycle escort around town, their care went further. On a visit to the notorious District Six market area they insisted on taking our wallets and passports and placing them in their own voluminous uniform jacket button-down breast pockets. One of them, 'Bokkie' said: "If you get the pocket picked, the wallet will be thrown over heads to another of the gang, and it will be a mile away in two seconds. No evidence, no crime eh?"

The Kruger Park was notable for an off-road bushland tour in a ranger's truck, accompanied by two uniformed African assistants. We got close up to lions, springbok, giraffe and very close to an apparently disgruntled elephant. The raised trunk, huge tusks and trumpeting led the white ranger to call from the cab to the open platform we rode on that "if necessary you can run up the kopje", a nearby hillock. "The jumbo can't follow. Too steep, eh man." Gratuitous advice, it was agreed among us on the truck tray. We just crouched down and hung on as it was backed slowly away.

We visited Soweto, the giant black African enclave outside Johannesburg that provided the work force for the white dominated society and its predominant mining industry. In fact at a shebeen, a bar cafe, we were offered and tasted some local mealie beer. I don't recommend it over a good cold Fosters lager.

I was visiting a pariah state, and it's an interesting footnote that my passport listing my occupation as journalist and with my employment effectively by the republic's Foreign Affairs Ministry, carried little weight. I was given a letter on landing at airport immigration stating what I could and could not do while visiting, with the written demand that the letter be surrendered on my departure.

I felt a sidebar story coming on and decided to 'lose' the missive instead, which I did by hiding it in a sock in my suitcase. No joy though. When I was about to fly out after three weeks of "everything paid for Mr Campbell" and brilliant Boer hospitality, food and beverages "we must have your admission letter sir." The plane was loaded out on the flight line and I was firmly refused permission to board without producing the letter, Discretion won and I managed to find it had somehow slipped to a sock, "so sorry." I was the last to board the plane stairway after being escorted by an official across the tarmac to an impatient cabin crew.

South Africa's apartheid policies were gaining in international criticism. I had mixed feelings as I had met, along with the ever present 'minder', one Habakuk Shikwane, a black African entrepreneur who employed hundreds of people in his cane furniture factory near Pretoria. He had a chauffeur-driven Mercedes and his children went to school in Switzerland. Our white government minder seemed proud to show him off as an example of racial accord. However post apartheid and over the Rubicon it became known that he was a communist and prominent member of the outlawed African National Congress. But at that time he appeared to support placing apartheid in a new light. Propaganda is a powerful tool, spun well.

On a more sobering note, I was also given a tour of the government nuclear power plant at Pelindaba. I recalled that clearly after it was reported later that a nuclear bomb blast had been monitored by a US satellite at a remote site in South West Africa which was a Pretoria protectorate.

But back in Canberra, I was absorbed in publishing *South African Review*, a 12 page glossy look at life in the country. I was also enjoying using the embassy Mercedes Benz with CD plates and the occasional diplomatic cocktail circuit. Where else would a 20-year-old Kiwi journo play in a working-day golf foursome with diplomatic staff including the South Korean information attache at the Royal Canberra Golf Club.

An incident at a National Press Club luncheon where I was guest at a diplomatic table gave me food for thought. I was seated next to a Russian envoy who, in squeezing a lemon onto his seafood cocktail, sprayed red sauce across my nice white shirt.

With apologies and a serviette treatment, I forgot the incident. Except that two days later, a Soviet messenger came up the path at my home address and presented me with two new high-quality boxed dress shirts, in my collar size. The Russians had tabs on things it seemed.

In April that year I celebrated my 21st birthday and the event was made raucous by my access courtesy of my attache boss, Koos Venter, to the diplomatic corps duty-free stores. Tax-exempt champagne was the order of the night and a shuttle service to the Canberra Hospital nurses home from our journo's rented suburban house, Hangovers were treated the next day at the main bar of the 'Wello' the Wellington Hotel near Parliament and a media watering hole.

CHAPTER FOUR

JOINING US WORKING journos often was one Rupert Murdoch, who arrived in town to launch his flagship venture *The Australian* newspaper a couple of years earlier. Rupert was perched on a bar stool with the rest of us, engaged in banter and job anecdotes, as 'one of the lads', before the rarified air of media mogul lifted him out of our common orbit as he went on to amass an empire. I guess he had a kick start with his dad leaving him a newspaper in Adelaide as a springboard to fame. Back then he was pretty much just another bloke and in fact, he canvassed some of us for his staff.

It was about this time after six months in the embassy role that I started getting job offers from mainstream Canberra media. Over a few beers one night, funnily enough poolside at a suburban motel where Bob Hawke, then a trade union activist – later to be Prime Minister – was holding court. I was firmly offered a position in the Federal Parliamentary Press Gallery with the domestic wire service *Australian United Press*. Indeed, there was an undertone that I was maybe working for the wrong masters where I was. There can be peer group pressure in many a profession and this probably made my decision to resign from the embassy world and head back to the craft proper. I still have a copy of my last *SA Review* complete with embassy staff farewell signatures.

Press gallery experience in the federal parliament was going to enhance any newsman's resume. It was impeccable timing too, as I soon had a front row seat at world-shaking news. At *AUP* I covered politics, with many days sitting in the high press balcony over the parliamentary debating chamber mindful that the MP speaking at that moment might be representing a corner of an Australian state containing one of our subscribing newspapers. In fact in summer, high under the corrugated iron roof of the old building it was helluva hot and some days we stripped to singlets in the news office, having to re-don our shirt and tie to take the few steps out onto the gallery proper. It was a busy time, as we had many masters that paid for *AUP*'s coverage. The job also had a great money-saving perk with cheap gourmet dinners, port and cheese etc. in the parliamentary dining room.

But then came a world news bombshell, just as we were exploring the possibility of a Christmas break. On December 17th 1967, Prime Minister Harold Holt, who liked a dip in the surf, disappeared while swimming at Cheviot Beach near Portsea in Melbourne.

With this event came a tsunami of news stories and speculation abounded as did bad jokes about Russian submarines, hungry sharks and the like. Some 24 hours after he entered the surf, Australia's Governor-General had to end Holt's commission. John McEwen 'Black Jack' to the media was sworn in as PM. Intensive media coverage followed and plans were laid for a memorial service.

The Vietnam War was raging, and one of the chief mourners proved to be US President Lyndon Baines Johnson, whom Holt had supported with Australian troop commitment and the slogan 'All the Way, with LBJ.'. Many other leaders including Charles, Prince of Wales, UK PM Harold Wilson, United Nations: UN boss U Thant, and of course New Zealand PM, Sir Keith Holyoake, were inbound from around the world for a service on December 22nd at St Paul's Anglican Cathedral, Melbourne.

On assignment to cover President Johnson when he visited Canberra to meet with Cabinet members, I was heartily shaken by the hand by LBJ as he arrived up the steps of the Canberra Rex Hotel and reached our waiting corps. Of course he was surrounded by his Secret Service minders and we were soon asked to provide one reporter and one photographer to cover his meeting in a conference room upstairs. This would be observation only, no interviews. Two of our number were quickly chosen by ballot and the reporter involved decided to throw in a question in the conference room. He afterwards described being seized from behind by the shoulder and hauled out of the room with the hissed admonition from the secret service minder "No words."

Like any series of stories in our world of news, events overtook the Holt drama at least from the front pages. It was only a couple of months later that I found myself covering the arrival of a fairytale potentate at the Royal Australian Air Force Fairbairn base for its security perimeter. Landing was the Emperor of Ethiopia, the Lion of Judah and a few other exotic superlatives, Haile Selassie, on a official visit, accompanied by his two daughters, Princesses Sofie Desta and the unpronounceable Ijigayehou

Assfa Wossen and sundry minor Ethiopian officials.

As usual, the niceties of diplomacy had no play in Aussie pragmatism and the Ethiopians had to step through a large metal tray of potassium permanganate, Condy's crystals solution at the foot of the aircraft steps as a precaution against the foot and mouth disease endemic in their homeland. It gave my colleague on the *Sydney Mirror* a great intro to his report over the phone to a copy-taker. "Haile Selasie, Lion of Judah, potentate of Ethiopia had to do the foot and mouth two-step before stepping onto Aussie soil today."

CHAPTER FIVE

SOON THOUGH THOUGHTS returned to points north and the urge to see new fields including Britain was still strong as the ultimate destination we had planned from New Zealand. At least Australia had improved the travel fund and as it happened, *AUP* provided an unexpected and strong opening. We were monitored in Sydney by the American-based *United Press International* wire service, and through this link I met one Charles Bernard, the bureau chief for Australia and a delightful Yank who occasionally visited Canberra on mysterious errands.

On one of these, we were talking shop early in 1968 and when I suggested *UPI* might have job openings overseas, particularly London, Charles was supportive. Back in Sydney he wrote to me: "You New Zealanders have such a good reputation with us overseas, I am sure everyone would look twice at your application." He could certainly provide assistance as a referee should it come to pass that I found myself in the area concerned.

My mate Trevor Hawkins – known also as Dean, his second name, had got married and seemed well settled as a result so I decided onward and upwards would be a good move. To boost my funds, I worked all hours available and lived simply at home, by-passing the Wello watering hole more often than was fair and soon booked passage with Qantas to London Heathrow on what was then dubbed the Kangaroo route.

Still well into the future were the marathon world-spanning flights of today and my 707 suffered an engine delay that gave me a complimentary night at the Sydney Hyatt while it was rescheduled. When it took off it carried my economy class seat to Perth, Singapore, Kuala Lumpur, Bahrain I think, Rome and London. With some 36 hours actually in the air mixed with airport stops I was somewhat tired and emotional by the time I was lugging a suitcase around Kensington High Street looking for a cheap room for rent. When I found something suitable, an unsympathetic landlady told me to cross the busy street to the house opposite which had a bath upstairs on the second floor. I chose bed and slept for a good 12 hours straight. When I investigated the bathroom option, it produced a gurgling brown liquid.

Fortunately I had some ex-Kiwi and Aussie contacts in the big city and a few phone calls from a pub offering warm beer on a nearby corner located them flatting in Earls Court which was notorious as an antipodean enclave and I was directed to a meeting at the Zambezi Club, a speakeasy redolent with the twangs of home and South Africa. The bar acted as a message exchange of sorts, and I soon had a couple of addresses seeking a rent share prospect. I soon settled into an upstairs flat conversion in a Fulham Palace Road terraced house mainly because it had a working shower!

With an interview pending with *UPI* I took a little time out and bought a bus pass that delivered me to such sights as the Tower of London, Hampton Court, Buckingham Palace of course and Hyde Park and

Fleet Street stopping for research purposes at the odd famous pub along the way. It was as well I took a little tourist time out because once I was seated at an acceptance interview with newsroom boss Greg Jensen at *UPI*'s Bouverie Street offices, just off Fleet Street, it was apparent that sweatshop time had arrived. I regarded a job with the agency as a major career step, as it opened up the world of a foreign correspondent. In just five short years I had landed a senior journalist's role in London, whereas if I had stayed on the *Daily News* promotion ladder, I would technically be in my first year as a junior reporter under the New Zealand grading system – with luck. At its peak, the agency had more than 2,000 full-time staff and 200 news bureaux in 92 countries and more than 6,000 media subscribers. But with opportunity came reality as before I could hope to see a line bureau somewhere in the world. I had a baptism in London working a roster of shifts covering 24 hours on the international desks, disseminating news that flowed in by teleprinter and cable from around the world. There was the Euro desk, the Middle East and Africa (Medaf) Desk, and the American Desk with each capping a line of bureau's feeding into them and then speeding these reports on to agency newspaper, TV and radio clients world-wide. But despite a huge international staff, on the European Desk in the British capital, just two journalist-editors controlled the news flow to and from Europe, the Middle East and Africa to the rest of the world on any one eight hour stint. Too often I worked the midnight to dawn graveyard shift, but because of the time zones involved, this was more often than not a time of major breaking news.

The senior staffer controlled the 'slot' clearing incoming copy from bureau and domestic wires and reassigning stories onwards to the outgoing wires as appropriate. Desk chairs were highly mobile on rolling wheels which eased the travel between banks of teleprinters surrounding the slot. Across the wide curving desk complex was the 'rim' where I was first stationed, with the job of editing and improving copy, rewriting truncated cable reports, sometimes using UPI code names. An example of this the code for New Zealand was appropriate as 'Agricolae'. Code was used in the reporting field to safeguard what might be important giveaways if copy was intercepted by competition media outlets. The job was not overly paid and I started on what was known as the Fleet Street Minimum at 25 quid a week, equivalent to about $900.00 in 2024 rates. Fortunately my efforts were recognised by London bureau chief Dan Gilmour with a couple of five pound increments as time passed.

CHAPTER SIX

As THE FIRST recipient of stories filed by line staffers and other domestic agencies, it was a ringside seat on world events, and one of my first was when on April 4th 1968, as I contemplated celebrating my 22nd birthday a few days later, Martin Luther King was shot dead on the balcony of his second-floor room at the Lorraine Motel in Memphis, Tennessee. As the story rolled over my desk on to European clients in the next days, racial riots claimed 40 lives in the US.

Beginning in May 1968, riots and strikes swept across France with reports coming in from correspondents flocking to the scene suggesting civil war was on the cards and we harried deskmen were kept busy telling the rest of the world, including when President de Gaulle did a runner to safety in Germany.

Story superseded story and then I suddenly found myself on my first UPI reporting assignment, in fact my first 'foreign correspondent' role, when Greg Jensen suggested that as I was a New Zealander, I must know about tennis. His logic escaped me, but loath to admit ignorance I stepped up and found myself in southwest London covering minor Wimbledon courts for low-seeded client interest. In fact, I picked up the scoring vernacular in the press room and managed to acquit myself reasonably well. But a more experienced sports writer from a line bureau arrived to report the central court events and final with Rod Laver winning the men's singles title as I watched from the press box.

Back on the desk, violence erupted closer to home in August that year when a loyalist parade in Derry, Northern Ireland sparked three days of rioting between Protestants and Catholics, and a divide that saw British troops arrive to control a virtual civil war on the streets that was to last for years. The Troubles, was a daily update for my whole time at the agency.

I was grabbing a cup of indifferent coffee when the teleprinters hummed into a series of bells that signalled us to an incoming 'bulletin' news break, a 'flash'. Sure enough in a world-changing move on August 20th, 1968, the Soviet Union invaded Czechoslovakia. A day later, this compiled report from London went over the international wires:

> PRAGUE, Aug. 21 1968 (UPI) – Invasion forces from Russia and its satellites occupied Czechoslovakia with troops, tanks and jet planes against sporadic resistance today and snuffed out the country's experiment in liberal reform. Street fighting in Prague left some dead and wounded as thousands of Czechoslovaks surged into the streets and shouted defiance of the invaders. Canon, machine-gun and small arms fire crashed and rattled through the night in the capital. Czechoslovak leaders denounced the invasion by Soviet, East German, Hungarian and Bulgarian mobile forces and demanded they pull out. Some Czechoslovaks tried to stop the invaders by throwing themselves in front of tanks in Prague's St. Wenceslas Square and outside the Radio Prague building. CTK news

agency reported 'several' persons had been killed and at least 57 others wounded. One report said 25 were killed. Radio Prague played the Czech national anthem and went off the air pleading 'no street fighting.' People ignored the plea. They began stalking and setting fire to Russian tanks. Burning mattresses were dropped from windows on two tanks and two Soviet ammunition trucks were ambushed and blown up.

Given the U.S. involvement in the accelerating Vietnam war, Russia reckoned they would get away with a purely European affair. President Johnson bailed out of a planned summit meeting with Soviet boss Leonid Brezhnev but that was it.

The Vietnam conflict was another daily update on the European desk, feeding stories off the US wire into the continent across the English Channel and with this task came a particular subbing language. American correspondents in Saigon had a hometown vernacular. The opposition to American forces were simply Reds, the US forces GI's requiring our substitution of Viet Kong or Hanoi regulars and US troops for European client consumption.

On perhaps a more prosaic news level came the tragedy for U.S. singing star Roy Orbison. He was on an appearance tour of England in September when the news hit our wires that his home in Tennessee had burned down and his two eldest sons had died in the blaze. Orbison was appearing in Birmingham and New York tasked London to find him. I kept my head down and looked busy as I had no desire to be the one to reach him with the news. As it was the British tabloid press had the news from UPI and soon had a local reporter at his hotel.

Al Webb was a colleague on the American desk and a veteran of front-line coverage of the Asian conflict. I once saw him dive under his desk when one of our group of locally employed, often Cockney, teleprinter operators, dropped a large metal bin of waste ribbon tape punched by the machines. The metal boomed as it hit the tiled floor, just like a bomb explosion and Al's reaction was instinctive from being in a combat zone. The operator was most amused but a further deliberate 'drop' earned him the threat of being fired if it happened again.

The US slot had a fair share of colourful characters, I suspect as a rest from the strains of front line reporting. One such was Dick Growald, US desk manager, a large man with a reinforced desk chair and a temper. "Godda . . . growl . . . Godamn . . . louder growl . . . Godamned mother fucking son of a bitch . . . growl and smashing his telephone handpiece on the edge of his desk until all that was left were two wires hanging out of broken plastic.

Al Webb, and I formed a friendship outside of the job which enlivened our days off, often three in a row after seven days on. Invariably this involved a dawn finish and what better than a few beers to wind down. As always, London had an answer and we would adjourn to Smithfield Meat Market where sides of beef and lamb and pigs were auctioned and sold for the forthcoming day's restaurant and butchery trade.

It had its specially licenced early morning pub and somehow journos from the nearby Fleet Street media circus had an honorary membership. We usually floated home on a bus or the tube to sleep well with plans for further days-off activity.

I formed what proved to be a life-long friendship with Mike Poole, a Brit on the Medaf Desk who had the use of his family's yacht and I had halcyon days in summer cruising as his deckie out of Buckler's Hard on the Beaulieu River running into the Solent.

With Al Webb, activity usually centred on matters bibulous and we frequented many a well known local, notably the Tipperary and the Red Lion, when we weren't partying at his or another colleague's flat. There is a particular memory of leaving a Fleet Street pub late one night and returning to work in narrow Bouverie Street to find a blue Rolls Royce parked half on the footpath. Opposite UPI was the *News of the World* and the Roller belonged to its new publisher, Rupert Murdoch, of my Canberra acquaintance, now dubbed 'the Dirty Digger' for his onslaught against the British press scene. He'd also bought *The Sun* into his expanding media empire. I took a certain delight, relieving a couple of pints and echoing local sentiment by pissing on his rear off-side wheel in the poorly lit street.

There was more sober and illustrious entertainment too. I snaffled a media pass to a Buckingham Palace Garden Party and actually met Queen Elizabeth II and Prince Phillip in a quickly moving lineup. I didn't know it then, but there was to be a longer encounter many years in the future.

On one occasion, a friend from one of the London papers had office tickets to a fund-raising special premiere of Sammy Davis Junior in *Golden Boy* at the London Palladium. This was notable because after a few relaxing beverages, we took a London cab to the show and stepped from the taxi onto a red carpet running out to the footpath. There was a smattering of applause from crowds behind velvet ropes watching for guest notables. We managed to keep straight faces, wave vaguely and stroll casually into the lobby, leaving a speculative gathering behind us on the footpath. It was a great show too, with a curtain call where Davis sat at the stage steps and chatted and sang some more.

Days off were an opportunity to do some exploring and Mike's Mini took us far afield in the lovely English countryside. We stayed a night with nice friends near Ipswich and I was fascinated by the long Viking barrows like small hillocks in otherwise flat fields. These were burial tombs, many long since plundered by well-meaning historians and earlier thieves no doubt. On that historical note, I also met a young lady who drove me on one occasion to Stonehenge. Back in those days, it was wide open to visit for free and we picnicked happily on one fallen monument. I retraced my steps in much later years to find the mysterious monument fenced off with tourist queues and ticket sales and figure I had the very best of the experience.

There was a hovercraft trip from Dover to Calais and a bus to Paris for the national Bastille Day 14th of July, an encounter with a lovely lady student from the Sorbonne and an intense French lesson. Another memorable evening was spent when friends from Canberra reunited in London and the next thing I knew a wedding was happening. The bride's father was a well-heeled Queensland grazier and his wedding contribution in absentia was a slap up multi-course French menu dinner, champagne, brandy and liqueurs for six wedding party expatriates in the Patience private dining room at the Savoy Hotel. It was tough at the top.

In fact the Savoy experience mentioned in a letter home rekindled a memory for my father, who had escaped from an Italian POW camp in 1943, made his way down Italy to meet incoming allied forces, and was eventually sent via Gibraltar to London. He had a contact on the Savoy staff who fixed him up in an attic servants quarters bed, in exchange for some samples from a bunch of bananas my Dad scored in Gibraltar. Great wartime currency.

CHAPTER SEVEN

LONDON PUBS WERE an experience in other ways during my time there. A fellow scribe at *UPI* was an Aussie, Peter Dyke, who had a flat at Bethnal Green a few steps from a pub called the Carpenter's Arms, then recently owned by the infamous Kray twins. Ronnie and Reggie, criminals and killers notorious in the thriving London underworld were arrested in 1968 and subsequently jailed for life. Bethnal Green was their home turf and they liked the Carpenters for its long bar and single door entrance where a watcher meant they could not be surprised. It still had a bullet hole in a wire-reinforced toilet window, kept as a talking point by the then managers. I still have their business card: 'Jean and Esty welcome you'. As antipodeans, we were pretty well regarded by pub regulars who had rubbed shoulders with the Krays and did their bidding no doubt. We were looked at as unlikely opposition crooks encroaching on their 'patch'. My friend Mike Poole later succeeded to Peter's flat and also had beers at the Kray's old HQ. He told me later "I really loved that area and the wildlife – there is nothing like an East End knees-up and the whole pub in full chorus."

I had an encounter too with the IRA. A favoured watering hole was the Tipperary in Fleet Street. History has it that it was London's first ever Irish pub, originally the Boars Head and rebuilt after the Great Fire of London in 1666. In a school of journos I once exchanged a few words with one Fred Forsyth, who was later to become rich with *The Day of the Jackal* among other good books. I heard shortly afterwards he had taken off to Biafra as a freelance writer, where a civil war was turning into genocide, more *UPI* material and I watched jealousy as one of my journo peers at work was sent off to report the conflict.

Towards the close of 1968, the pub manager was due off on holiday to Ireland and on the lookout for a relief barman. I was just going on four weeks annual leave, but was a little short of funds. I volunteered to run the upstairs Doubles Bar with wage and keep for three weeks. By then I could well afford a week travelling. So it was, but after just a couple of days, I came down from the third floor residence to find the ground floor poker machine prised open with a kitchen carving knife, an empty cash register and some bare spirit shelves. The ground floor public barman and current assistant manager, subsequently located in Belfast, seemed to have escaped into the protection of the outlawed Irish Republican Army. The brewery that owned the pub sent in a new interim manager after I rang the cops and spent an interesting day fielding phone calls from various Fleet Street reporters on why the pub wasn't open on time, a major matter of importance to the press pack. I finished my time at the bar upstairs and happily wandered off with friends to Wales and Cornwall for a week's holiday.

The arrival of 1969 foreshadowed a bit of a news storm according to my sporadically entered diary. It was snowing in London when the new US President-elect Richard M. Nixon swore the oath of office in Washington on January 20th, with the promise of ending the grinding attrition of the Vietnam War. It wasn't to be, but talks on the conflict between U.S. and North Vietnam began in Paris to add to the content on *UPI* wires, with staff flitting in and out of watching progress in Paris. In his first months in office, Nixon directed the U.S. military to increase its pressure on the battlefield, while ordering the secret B–52 bombings of North Vietnamese base camps in Cambodia.

Mike Poole remembers:

> "Vietnam war. Copy in from the US. The Pentagon had decided to 'liberalise the protective reaction strike policy'. I turned to Al, veteran of Vietnam reporting, who was manning the US slot. 'What does this mean Al?' Bit of a chew on the thought. Then in a lovely slow drawl – 'guess it means they're going to bomb the crap out of Cambodia.' Next day they did."

History would show it took until 1973 to make any peace progress Nixon had intended. Unfolding anecdotes from Paris revealed a side of the job that only the naive would have doubted, with pub talk referring to early morning hotel room meetings reported between some newsmen and members of the American and North Vietnamese official delegations. With its huge international sweep, UPI was an obvious source of information denied the average domestic news operation. It was a certainty that the Central Intelligence Agency had a number of UPI cover identities scattered through the network, but the purposes of these pages is an account of the Fourth

Estate and not of associated intelligence gathering.

The opposition to the war continued to increase with more and more people from all walks of life attending anti war demonstrations and demanding that the US withdrew from Vietnam. The music came from groups including The Doors, Led Zeppelin, Janis Joplin and the Beatles and many others.

In the now legendary Concert in Hyde Park, I listened as The Rolling Stones Mick Jagger marked the death of group member Brian Jones in a swimming pool days earlier, reciting from Adonais, a poem by Shelly 'peace peace he is not dead, he hath awakened from the dream of life'. As he intoned to a packed and silent crowd of many thousands 3,000 white butterflies were released from the stage. I was rather pleased to see my story make a space on the front page of the *International Herald Tribune* in Paris, for one.

There were other major news events rolling through the year, sometimes snowballing into each other. Apart from the ongoing conflicts and political sidebars of the Vietnam war and the Troubles across the Irish Sea we covered the first Concorde supersonic jet taking off in France and arrival of the Boeing 747 that then revolutionised air transport across the globe.

On July 20th 1969, one of man's crowning achievements occurred when American Neil Armstrong became the first human to set foot on the Moon and uttered the immortal "That's one small step for [a] man, one giant leap for mankind." We watched this flickering black and white television coverage in the newsroom and it provided an object lesson in creative news coverage. Euro desk manager Greg Jensen had sourced the whole plan for the moon landing, written all the copy ready for release if everything went to plan and included features on special aspects. He released this consecutively onto the wires as we watched the action unfold on the office TV. His foresight and preparation succeeded in beating the US home coverage from mission HQ. A very professional job.

Covering war and famine as a regular job should harden most reporters but I defy anyone to claim ambivalence in cases of gruesome murder. Cold horror was my reaction to a bulletin flash from Los Angeles one night in August that actress Sharon Tate who was eight-and-a-half months pregnant had been slaughtered with four other victims in a home invasion by cult followers of crazed self-styled guru Charles Manson.

UPI's Los Angeles bureau reported Tate's husband, director Roman Polanski, was in London and I found myself on the telephone ringing top hotels. I am pretty sure it was the Hilton when a night manager confirmed Polanski's 'manager' was in while the director was out at dinner. I spoke to an individual who said he could get a message to him. Unwilling to say more to a stranger, I simply said he needed to contact 'home' as soon as possible. I do not know the outcome of that message, but a subsequent call discovered a mob of British media had laid siege to the hotel and it was reported Polanski had collapsed on hearing the news. I was admonished by a seasoned UPI hack that I should have got a quote from my first contact anyway. But perhaps I had not hardened up to say "Sharon Tate has been slaughtered. What do you feel about that." I probably never will either.

Perhaps the murders were a catalyst to increasing thoughts of home on my part, having been away four and a bit years, or it may have been when getting into autumn with winter ahead I just had itchy feet. Letters from home included one from my sister Jan who was enamoured of a pirate radio station, Radio Hauraki, which was trying to break the New Zealand government monopoly on broadcasting. Staid dirges on state radio were only relieved with the odd weekly commercially sponsored half-hour hit parade of popular tunes. Radio Hauraki's pirates in a leaky old boat moored in international waters off the coast of Auckland were sending out hits of the day, many gleaned monitoring more liberal Australian stations across the Tasman Sea.

Jan sent me a cable asking if I could get hold of a record called *Where do you Go to My Lovely* by a Peter Sarsted. It was most certainly playing in London and the lyrics on a poor-born girl, Marie-Claire growing into top society, struck huge international success.

I quickly bought a copy and delivered it to a holidaying New Zealand airline pilot who was about to fly home. Two days later, it was thrilling Kiwi audiences on the Hauraki illicit frequency.

A combination of factors then unsettled my busy life. The UPI desk job was becoming onerous with shift work. There was the prospect of a line bureau job but it was probably going to be in Oslo at that time. The glamour postings pretty much went to American staff with the home market in mind. When I checked, Oslo was colder than the UK, and beer was three times the British price, along with the overall cost of living. There would be a language difficulty as I had only brushed up on my schooldays French with an eye to a Paris prospect. It was not an attractive proposition and if taken it would certainly extend my OE for years to come. Then a letter arrived from Radio Hauraki pirate entrepreneur David Gapes. A broadcasting licence was in the works from a government beleaguered by public opinion and jobs would be available if I was interested. The new medium had increasing interest and came at the right time. The one thing that really bugged me about the Brits was their visa rules for Commonwealth citizens. I had to renew my visa after two years, which involved spending a whole bloody afternoon in a queue at the Home Office surrounded by lovely people from India, Turkey, Bangladesh and sundry other countries seeking the right to stay in the cold and rain that was so often the climate. I had a sense of misguided entitlement I reckon because after all, my father had served with the RAF and helped defend the Poms. But this cut no ice of course, so I didn't actually try it on. Instead I thought bugger queuing all day, and to hasten the story, I resigned. I was though asked by Greg Jensen one more time "wanna reconsider NZ?" after I wrote a well received feature surrounding an unsuccessful move for the London wharf suburb called the 'Isle of Dogs' to secede from Britain. I had walked into the area for breakfast at a workers cafe after night shift and wrote an evocative background piece "It is just past dawn in the Isle of Dogs" highlighting poverty and slum life.

In February 1970 I bade farewell to many friends at the odd pub and party and sniffled on a girlfriend's shoulder, but booked passage on the Chandris Lines SS Australis from Southampton to Auckland. The sailing date was a month away, so I headed for Europe and took a train from Paris to Rome.

CHAPTER EIGHT

I BOOKED A wagon-lit, a sleeping car and armed with a baguette jambon – bread and ham and cheese – and a bottle of cheap but palatable French wine, I set off for the first part of the 12-hour journey seated by a window looking out as dusk fell over the flat countryside outside the Gare Austerlitz terminal. The sleeping car next door was lit up as night fell, and I was ready for my bunk when with an electric crackle and buzz, the lights went out. A conductor turned up and I was asked to move to the next car and take one of the four fold-out shelf-like sleepers. There wasn't room to undress so I covered myself with the blanket provided and soon drifted off. As dawn came, I stirred and rolled over to examine my surroundings. I found I had slept some 24 inches away from a nun in the foldout opposite! The French woman sat on her sleeper in full habit and offered me a polite 'bonjour' and a pleasant smile.

Rome in the morning promised a cool day ahead. Before leaving London I had joined the International Youth Hostels Association and waving my membership card at a station information office soon had me and my back-pack on a designated bus that dropped me at a hostel on the outskirts of town half-an-hour later.

While only a few lira, there was a three night limit, a 10pm curfew and closure between 10am and 4pm. I spent the rest of that day back in the city, visiting the Spanish Steps and Trevi fountain and dining on thick slices of pizza at a standup lunch bar. The following day it was off to the Colosseum and other landmarks including queuing for the Sistine Chapel. A day spent walking the city found me ready for sleep at the hostel that night with another plan forming. My father had been a prisoner of war at Modena in Italy after being shot down in the sea while flying out of Greece over Albania. He escaped the camp when the Italians bailed on the war, climbing over a back fence, while Germans came through the front gate as the Italian commandant turned a Nelsonian eye. Major Cargiolli had been a reluctant keeper of Allies and after the war he was often invited to returned services functions by his former charges including one in New Zealand. My father had given me his name as a lawyer in Florence, so I decided to look the gentleman up.

I took a train, found a much nicer hostel, and cold-called on an 'advocat' office. I soon learned that Signor Cargioli was actually in South Africa at another war vet reunion. However, the accommodating lawyer had his secretary make some phone calls and before I had finished a glass of chianti with my helpful legal chap, there was a knock on the door and a warm greeting from a very attractive woman about my own age. Things were looking up. Francesca Cargioli was the Major's daughter. Outside was parked her little red Innocenti, an Italian Mini and I was soon whisked at terrifying speed through narrow streets and up into nearby hills to the family villa just outside town. There in a black and white tiled reception room she indicated on a wall a framed collective photo of wartime allied forces prisoners where I soon pointed out my father at the end of one row. I received an enthusiastic hug and felt a response was in order, But we were interrupted by a uniformed chap who it turned out was the butler, bearing a supper of artichoke hearts and other delicacies. Another case of things being tough at the top.

The next few days were a blur of Innocenti jaunts around town. lunch at the old bridge, the Ponte Vecchio, visits to the art masterpieces in the Uffizi Gallery, a climb up the spiral internal wall staircase of Il Duomo and a visit to the classic Michelangelo grotto. Wines and pasta in country trattoria and also long conversations parked overlooking the River Arno saw me become very close to me accepting her invitation to find a job in Italy. Did she mean settle down as well? The prospect was not without attraction. We sort of decided I would have to continue with my planned voyage home, but with full intentions to look at the future. It is with some regret I look back on this interlude, but good sense has a way of working out. I don't think I was really destined for life in Italy and years of pasta and its results.

At the youth hostel I met an American couple heading for Switzerland in a Volkswagen sedan and looking to share petrol and expenses. Off we went staying in hostels for three days travel via the Leaning Tower at Pisa, up to Milan and across the Brenner Pass. The Swiss have wiener schnitzel and chips down to an art form where we lunched at Peter Sarsted-lauded St Moritz. We crossed into Germany, Munich beer halls, then into Holland and I farewelled my ride companions and took a train to The Hague and a ferry to Harwich in UK. After a day or so collecting bits and pieces stored with a friend, I took a train from Paddington to Southampton and my ship southwards.

The voyage was mainly notable for the fact that the morning after we sailed, we were northward at Den Hague which I had left just days before. It turned out that Chandris Lines had a contract to load assisted migrants for Australia. After these crowded aboard, the ship sailed for Tenerife in the Canary Islands, and welcome sunshine.

However rough weather opposite the Bay of Biscay led to social disaster, with hundreds of very seasick people from landlocked European communities turning ablution facilities into cesspools and complete no-go areas. A group of us who'd paid full fares for the voyage were soon given a designated closed toilet and shower facility. Apart from that, we settled into a routine of morning bouillon on the promenade deck, rather good meals, such as lots of crayfish after restocking at Cape Town where I briefly revisited South African soil. There were many captive nights in a lounge dancing to a Filipino cover band where every night ended to the strains of Proud Mary.

I remembered lines from the Ancient Mariner whispered in the ear of a young Kiwi lady who joined me in a shipboard romance that sadly only lasted until disembarkation in New Zealand and travel to opposite ends of the country. Our ship was followed for a week by a giant southern royal albatross hovering astern in the slipstream across many miles of the Indian Ocean. Landfall came at Perth, then Melbourne and finally

Auckland where my parents and two of three sisters were in the welcoming crowd at quayside.

CHAPTER NINE

RADIO HAURAKI, MY prospective employer, was granted a broadcasting licence in March 1970, after six years of illegal seaborne adventures. The move ashore would require a great reorganisation from pirate days when broadcasting law compliance always met a rude gesture and this was expected to take until later in the year involving premises to find, regulation equipment for broadcasting to install including a transmission mast and a myriad other legal details. In the intervening months I needed to earn a living. The Auckland waterfront was recommended by family friends in the know, and I found lucrative casual work as a 'seagull' tally clerk. In a time when cargo was shipped in freighters and was manhandled ashore with the lift of cranes, containers were still in the future at the port.

I would thus sit somewhere with a sight of the cargo hold to note down the loads going out by crane for 'the tally'. Occasionally there would be a concentration of 'wharfies' around a section of the hold and I was to see the odd cardboard carton leaving the ship looking a little tattered. This happened when some cartons were full of Japanese-export fishing reels. But I was prepared for such incidents and on a signal from my fellow workers I made the notation 'broken open in stow' in my tally. I had also been made aware of the fact that any thoughts of doing otherwise could result in a crane hook swinging where it should not. Accidents were not unknown when moving cargo ashore and I took great care not to be any sort of statistic.

In the meantime a colleague and another lifelong good friend, Adrian Blackburn was reporting for the *New Zealand Herald*, in those days an old-school and much respected masthead. He had closely followed the major developments in the Hauraki story, and with his kind permission I used his own words to background the new step into radio news journalism I was soon to take. The saga is very much a major story in it's own right, as Adrian's foreword in his excellent book *Radio Pirates* indicates:

> Just how extraordinary was the saga of the young pirates of Radio Hauraki and their struggle in the late 1960s to overcome a stifling uncreative state broadcasting monopoly'. The perspective offered by more than four decades in which private radio ventures in New Zealand have built on and profited from Radio Hauraki's final breakthrough provides the chance to assess the pirates achievement. Their persistent courage against overwhelming odds, with desperate financial problems a constant backdrop to their struggles against the government and officialdom, as well as the shipwrecks caused by some of the worst storms of the century, remains one of the great David and Goliath stories. Possibly even more significant though was their brash readiness to take on the establishment and all its forces in an era when making waves was not done, became a symbol for many thousands

of young New Zealanders of their personal potential for liberation and a more open New Zealand.

In fact revolution was still in the air and with the station about to go to air, I joined a dozen other journalists, many of them refugees from the staid government radio network, to be introduced to the prospects ahead. Dave Gapes and his fellow executives, including station manager and chief announcer Ian Magan briefed us thus:

Radio Hauraki will have the services of AP Reuter, the most comprehensive available in New Zealand. Overseas news will be broadcast up to one hour before the government stations. In addition to a completely independent national radio news service now being established, our newsman will fly by light aircraft to any part of New Zealand to cover major news stories in depth. Wellington journalists will provide exclusive background – on local news we will make the utmost use of modern technology as well as top newsmen to give Auckland its most effective ever local news coverage, light aircraft broadcasting traffic reports, radio equipped news cars will put our reporters on the air with the news as it happens. This new service is an ambitious project and it has a big budget, the biggest item of expenditure on Radio Hauraki, and most important of all, the right people.

Heady stuff indeed back in 1970 and I can confirm

the promise made was certainly kept for many years until communications technology consigned such commitment to history.

On Saturday, September 26th 1970, Ian Magan flicked the switch opening his microphone in brand new studios in Auckland's downtown Caltex House and began a countdown to 6am to launch the first legal private radio station in New Zealand's history. So began a new adventure and those heady days were captured later by my first day colleague, now long-serving Kiwi journalist and now author, Tom Clarke who recalls:

> The excitement of the amazing adventure that was Radio Hauraki still feels as good today as it did in 1970. Venturing into the wild world of ex-pirate radio alongside a bunch of madly enthusiastic youngsters of my own vintage, 24 at the time, was not only exhilarating, but it was thrilling beyond my wildest imaginings. We had some great journalists amongst the staff, which I recall numbered 24. There was a tremendous thrill that went from being in the best newsroom in the country.
>
> Amongst the highlights in terms of people, was my yachting buddy Mike Brockie, who later went on to fame at another New Zealand commercial news innovator, TV3. Our emphasis back then was on fast, accurate reporting of news, and we scored some amazing coups in those early days.
>
> Radio Hauraki was the ultimate employment

enjoyment. We were having such a ball of a time. And that's not to even think about the wonderful young ladies who used to cover reception duties outside the newsroom door, who used to delight in summertime in appearing in Carnaby Street fashions, Great days I will never forget – nor will I ever forget the enthusiasm and the sheer enjoyment of working in such a positive, innovate and impactful environment.

Tom would go on to reconnect with me in broadcasting in our more senior years, still aglow with his memories.

Another incident saw a newsman becoming the news, when a distressed radio car call came through the office monitor. Newsguy Rick Mayne remembers: "I was in the Hauraki white Mini news car stopped at a red light at the corner downtown of Swanson and Queen about 11am. Lots of construction work was going on outside. Suddenly the roof of the car implodes about three or four inches from the left side of my head...a worker on the sixth floor had dropped a three metre length of rebar and it speared through the Mini's roof. I was ok, uninjured but what the fuck? I thought! People milling about, even a TV crew shooting some vision for that night Radio Hauraki boy reporter becomes the news!"

In my own case I manned the news sub's desk and before long found myself before a microphone to read a bulletin live on air. I was clammy with sweat on that first occasion, and in retrospect must have sounded like a vinyl record played at high speed in an effort to put drama and excitement into what I was imparting to the million listening ears I imagined out there.

It was an incompetent apprenticeship that did not last long as with a little coaching from more experienced announcing staff and with a huge input from my dear younger sister Jan, an ex-pirate then heading the station's advertising copywriting team, it became second nature even on a breakfast shift at 6am after a late night out beforehand, although Gapes might comment with a sideways look, about a 'gravelly voice'

It wasn't long though before the new-found broadcasting freedom translated into a hazing approach at times. On one occasion I had a six page news bulletin rushed into the news booth at the last minute and I opened the link and read the lead story only to find the second stapled together with the remaining pages. I managed to keep reading, which required a little ad-libbing "and just to hand a late item has been handed to me" while managing to prise the staple apart and continue. It didn't happen a second time, but there was also the odd Saturday night shift when I for one was suddenly faced mid-sentence with a vivacious receptionist lass suddenly lifting her top and pressing the result against the glass of the news reading booth, Most disconcerting. It became a point of honour to not miss a beat in the broadcast when such untoward incidents occurred now and then.

The pirate heritage was actively encouraged in the station's overall image with a promotional utility vehicle transformed into a mock ship's bridge over the cab in miniature as a salute to the early days. In an organised city welcoming parade along Auckland's Queen Street with Her Majesty Queen Elizabeth 11 seated on the official dias, we Hauraki staff rode on the ute dressed as pirates and waving wooden swords. Such was the irreverence we displayed that one of our reporters, Huw Patterson, was distributing pamphlets on the station to the watching crowd and somehow managed to deliver one into Her Majesty' hands as he made his way past. A republican equality of manner prevailed.

There was a vibrant social life involved in working for what was the premier rock'n'roll 'top of the dial' broadcaster. Saturday night shifts were inundated with telephoned invitations to parties where the station's music offerings were centre stage. But there was also a serious side pretty much carried by the newsroom.

My first major story was to enter the New Zealand history books after a South Auckland farmer Arthur Allan Thomas was found guilty of the murder of his neighbours Jeanette and Harvey Crewe. With the verdict, a major campaign was launched at a meeting I attended over a bicycle repair shop in the Auckland suburb of Onehunga, where Thomas's family and supporters vowed to prove his innocence. I remember being impressed with their arguments. l would later be justified as it took retrials and appeals and investigations, including strong evidence of a corrupt police detective, over almost a decade behind bars before Thomas was eventually pardoned. No one else has ever been brought to book for the murders.

But in the way of the world, bad news, the worst

of news overshadows all else and so it was when my beloved mother fell to the ravages of cancer, opening a new perspective on my heretofore carefree, if selfish, life. I had just become used to the loss and a renewed closeness with my father and I sharing the family home, when in an almost insurmountable grief fell over us, an overwhelming tragedy when my beloved sister Jan was killed in a car crash.

It was a double fatality with Jan's work colleague and friend Lindzi Draper also killed as the car in which they were travelling for a weekend away hit another vehicle head-on near the town of Huntly.

The crash had made a police news item that I had read to air shortly after the accident with few details other than a fatal road crash had occurred. It was not until I pulled into the car park of the local Press Club after my shift and later that night, that I was met by the station boss Dave Gapes and Ian Magan and others who were obviously looking for me. I heard the dreadful details then. Somehow, after telling my father, older married sister and fielding telephone calls, I got through the ensuing days to a huge funeral event and then went back to work. One of my first new bulletins contained further details of an award Jan had won not long before that accident. To quote a local newspaper report:

> Jan Campbell is the girl who writes those ads on Radio Hauraki. She does it well too! A series she did on drugs has put her into world class Jan, 22, learned last week she had won an International Broadcast and Ideas Bank Award

involving competitors from radio stations in the USA, Canada and five top Australian networks. Entries were judged at an IBA conference in Canada. She wrote her Drug Abuse Campaign in four days plus 'a lot of thinking about it at home.' There were five spots ranging from 10 to 15 seconds "I do not really know much about drugs so it might have been a fresh approach. I put it in fairly plain language." She said the campaign was aimed at the North American market, dealing with hard drug problems not found in New Zealand. "I had a lot of literature to work from dealing with the effects of drugs, some of it was frightening." Jan has been a copywriter for Radio Hauraki for four years, the station's Managing Director Mr. David Gapes said last week. "We are all very proud of her. It's a great achievement." Was he going to give her a pay rise? "She's already one of the highest paid girls in advertising," he said.

I remember the ads punch-line set to a music sting – "Goddam the pusher man". In fact I was warned of the news item in case I wanted to stand down from that bulletin, but, I was proud of her success and wanted to help share it.

CHAPTER TEN

BUT PERHAPS NOT surprisingly, I had little appetite or real interest in the often mundane details of other lives and events, and before long I took a break. My father had led the way on a similar holiday staying with friends on Great Barrier Island, 50 miles off the coast.

The Island had been home for the pirate Radio Hauraki for six years at sea. In truth, much of that time had been spent tied up to the wharf at Okupu in Blind Bay, ready to sail at a moment's notice with word of an impending government inspector's appearance.

I flew to the island to spend a week with the hospitable O'Toole family in an isolated farmhouse. In between shooting my first wild pig, fishing for bountiful snapper and just plain relaxing, I explored the island. At Okupu, I found a property for sale. There was a rather dilapidated house and 12 acres adjacent to the wharf and on the foreshore was an old clinker-built lifeboat with Tiri 11, the name of the radio pirate vessel, painted across her stern.

Call it an omen and to shorten some detail, a group of friends and my father and I raised the purchase price between us and some months later, I farewelled Radio Hauraki and found a new life catching crayfish for a year. As a continuing connection to the Hauraki story, we had the old radio telephone system off the pirate ship to augment our party line telephone system, with its two lines from the local island exchange through to the mainland. It's a story with some fictional enhancement I related in part in a novel I penned in later years – *City of Storms*, still to be found on Amazon.

In the book is an account of a sperm whale stranding in 1972. I awoke one morning to see distant black objects on a beach at the head of Blind Bay. Taking a boat across from our mooring in front of the house, we soon realised there was a massive stranding of whales. Islanders quickly gathered but trying to save the giants was an impossible task. There were 14 carcasses in the end, one of them a huge bull on an adjacent beach with a small headland dividing the two strandings. After a nightmare of putrefaction in the wind for several days the Marine Department arrived from Auckland and set to work to tow the dead whales far out to sea. Before this some jaws and teeth were removed by local people and I wear a pendant of one tooth today. The bull on the second beach was actually buried with the help of a mechanical digger and many years later, an oil stain still appeared on the sand on a hot summer's day. From my book:

> Deep in the Ross Sea a 30 tonne sperm whale cruises north through icy waters to warmer breeding grounds. With his reference point a narrow mountainous land rising between the Pacific Ocean and the Tasman Sea, the huge bull is escorted by cows and calf offspring and the pod moves leisurely over silent days and mysterious nights along the rocky eastern coastline of New Zealand, instinctively following a centuries old sea lane. Then with

the mainland below the horizon on the left, and rugged, isolated Great Barrier Island veering away to the right, something fails. The great bull and his entourage end an ocean traverse by turning east into thrashing confusion on wide Okupu beach on Great Barrier Island's aptly named Blind Bay that leads nowhere. The senseless touch of land becomes a devil's anvil. The white sand emerges quickly from the receding tide, stranding the bull, the cows and calves on simmering sands, capped by a cloudless sky and scorching sun. Low water soon seals the trap and the mountains of flesh begin to slowly bake alive.

That tragedy aside, the island interlude somewhat cleared the head and I discovered that catching crayfish did not translate into lots of money in the bank and commercial success. In those days transport links with the mainland by air and sea were sporadic and often delayed by bad weather, and this led to intermittent sales. But it was a great life and finally I felt recharged to get back to the news business. Radio Hauraki welcomed me back and my new found wife, Denise, was soon working alongside on the station reception desk and in other staff assistant roles.

Around this time, I helped create an underwater live radio broadcast which I believe was a world first, if not the only such event ever.

A friend of the station owned a company called Diver Services and had acquired lightweight helmets equipped with microphones, designed to allow divers to talk to the surface while doing underwater ship hull inspections. Why not link that communication system with a transmitter and relay it through Radio Haurali's airwaves I thought? Better still, put a well known announcing personality, a Hauraki Good Guy, underwater to do the honours. I put the idea to our top breakfast DJ, Fred Botica, and he was all for it. Thus a small fleet of launches set out one Saturday equipped with tech experts from the station, and Ian Magan as boss. Fred and I went under the sea a mile or two offshore, and it all came together. We described our impressions and the sea floor, the odd fish and an empty beer bottle half buried in the sand to add conservation and pollution to the message successfully broadcast live across the mainland. Technician Graham Browne recalls:

> I remember this O.B.(outside broadcast). We used a VHF FM radio link. The setup was audio from the diver comms unit patched into a Shure portable mixer then into the link. We did do most of the broadcast but I think it crapped out before the end when something happened with the diver unit. Overall it was considered a success.

In fact the fault was not mechanical but a Botica nose bleed, not conducive to breathing in a mask underwater. Fred was lifted aboard the boat with a watery boost from yours truly to end the adventure.

Another broadcasting innovation came with the arrival of an American hot-air balloonist who offered his services in a flight over the city. We quickly decided on a live broadcast from the high-flying wicker basket and announcer Jim Smith volunteered to fly. He did a series of crosses to the duty announcer from a portable VHF transmitter and it was an attention grabber for the Hauraki audience who also called in on the balloon appearing over their part of town. The only glitch came when it came time to land. What appeared to the pilot to be a clear patch of nice-looking grass was actually the Owairaka Bowling Club. He landed in a break in a major women's bowling tournament, rather digging up the turf in the process. However, the ladies were only too pleased to pour the intrepid airmen a cup of tea, while we ground support people organised a pickup and evacuation.

In August 1974, Prime Minister Norman Kirk died from heart failure at the age of just 51 and his untimely demise had an extra poignancy as his popularity had been saluted by the song *'Big Norm'* by the group Ebony, that was on the Hauraki playlist and on national charts. I flew to Wellington to cover the Lying in State at Parliament House, with live calls into the Fred Botica breakfast programme planned. All went well, despite a self-inflicted glitch after a late night catch up with fellow scribes at a local watering hole. When I was called for the morning crossover with Fred, I was still abed in my hotel room. But I grabbed the morning Post newspaper and after a quick glance managed to ad lib the fact that "hundreds of mourners are already gathering on the steps of Parliament house and officials expect the number to grow to thousands as the morning goes on" etcetera, for all the world as though I was live on the steps myself. Radio reporting has positional advantages.

Other Hauraki memories include interviews with singer Matt Munroe, whose track *'Born Free'* was the station's chosen signature tune, as well as Elton John, Rick Wakeman and other lesser local mortals. Ian Magan ran a concert company and in 1978, he booked top star Chuck Berry to play two dinner shows at a downtown cabaret, with Hauraki staff invited along. I had a bird's eye balcony view of a drama when Berry did a runner after his first show and Magan chased him out an exit door after being told Berry, who had been pre-paid, was headed to the airport. Magan headed off in pursuit and tried to get Berry arrested at Auckland airport but had no documentation with him to enforce his claim. He said after the incident:

> Chuck just stood there, knowing there was nothing anyone could do. Once they called his flight, he just turned on his heel and took off through the departure gate. That's the last I ever saw of the man.

CHAPTER ELEVEN

MARRIAGE FOR ME was certainly a sea change and for whatever reason we decided that travel together might be a good start to settling down more effectively so I sent off a note to *The Canberra Times*, my old employer and soon had the offer of a position along with a company flat ready and waiting. This seemed like a good opportunity and we flew off to Canberra in late 1974 and I found myself on the sport's section of the sub's desk for whatever reason. Perhaps I had mentioned covering Wimbledon albeit very briefly. However I soon became conversant with Aussie Rules footy and various other sporting pursuits while Denise found herself on the reception desk of The Canberra Hotel dealing with itinerant VIP's MP's and various political lobbyists. It was a pleasant interlude marred by an apparent miscarriage event and after six months or so, we felt the need for a reason lost to time to return to New Zealand after all.

Marriage is not a very easy institution to be involved in, so life was a mix of energies directed domestically at home and then at work for some months with the New Zealand Broadcasting Corporation, the NZBC, in its Auckland studios serving radio stations 1ZB and 1ZM. It was drone work after the effervescence of private rock radio, but it paid the bills as I cast around for my next move. It came in an advertisement for staff in Asia. Now that was a new frontier and Radio Television Hong Kong's logo leapt off the newspaper employment page.

Off went my application and after a few weeks I was summoned to an interview by the Hong Kong Government's Auckland Consul. In 1974 the Crown Colony was British territory with all the red tape that involved. As it happened, I was full of flu and my hastily produced news reading sample tape was damning evidence of that fact. But ex Radio Hauraki's cachet was in effect. The radio staff advisor to said Hong Kong Consul and present for the interview was my old boss and close colleague, Ian Magan. He obviously spoke well of my ability because after another few weeks (I was to find nothing happened fast where Her Majesty's Government – HMG was concerned) a letter of appointment and paid travel instructions arrived. We flew Qantas with a Sydney stopover necessary it seems for her to buy clothing for Hong Kong. On we flew to Manila in the Philippines which was then a strip in a large flat plain dotted with the odd buffalo. In a humid rather rundown colonial-era terminal we lined up to reboard and were body-searched by a uniformed and rather attractive young lady soldier. I am not sure why this was necessary for passengers in transit, but had no real objection to the searcher.

Some 90 minutes later we landed at Kai Tak in Hong Kong, and experienced the final zooming 45 degree bank in to the runway between high rise apartment buildings bedecked with TV aerials and bamboo washing poles. Descending the stairs rolled out to the parked 707 we were greeted by humidity and the pungent smell of sewage from a nearby drainage canal, an introduction to a city redolent of odours, some good, many bad but which added up to an atmosphere I shall just describe as Asian exotic.

Passports stamped and we were met by a chap from Radio Hong Kong by the exotic name of Tiger Hussein and driven to the Holiday Inn among the neon glow of Tsim Sha Tsui's Nathan Road. There a spacious suite with all meal expenses was home for some six weeks, as I got to grips with the new job and we acclimatised, explored housing options and then applied for permanent government accommodation. It goes without saying that Hong Kong was a shock to the senses and a totally alien culture that took many weeks to settle into. But numerable trips on the Star Ferry and geographic familiarity along with guiding contact from long-time expatriate residents including several Kiwi colleagues in media jobs eased our settlement.

We considered ourselves fortunate to be allocated a four bedroom, two bath 3,000 square-foot brand new third floor apartment in a high rise complex, Baguio Villas, complete with a servants quarters and bathroom out back of the kitchen. Its large balcony barbecue area overlooked the South China Sea and Lamma Island to the west of Hong Kong Island. Denise was soon busy ordering government supplied standard furniture and adding home-making touches while I continued to work 12-hour shifts.

It became fairly obvious in my first weeks into a two-and-a-half year government contract that it was going to be a hard row to hoe after my past experience. I soon found the colonial administration epitomised an arrogant attitude. HMG ruled the roost in this last outpost of empire. It seemed to also be a refuge for old and tired civil servants dredged from tenure in British losses like India and Swaziland. Most of them had 'permanent and pensionable' status, so ability was not a job requirement. On top of that many government jobs went to long serving incumbents. In the case of Radio Hong Kong the news boss was a local man, a former teleprinter operator for Reuters who put his hand up when the station was upgraded. Presumably the name Reuters was all that mattered when staff were appointed. It was wholly based on the colonial concept of the BBC and for an ex Radio Hauraki newsman, it was like stepping decades into the past. I was employed on the sub's desk at Broadcast Drive in Kowloon, so named for the media outlets based in its single-entrance circular roadway, easily defended in case of local unrest, which encompassed Commercial Radio, Television Broadcasts and RTHK, all having English and Chinese broadcasting studios. I'll sum up the arrogance of colonialism by recalling a reprimand for using a red pen when marking wire copy to be typed up as a bulletin – to be read on air by a designated British accented announcer – not by me. A New Zealand accent was not suited to our listeners. Using red ink was the sole prerogative of the Governor, I was instructed! And what's more, hand subbing of wire copy accepted as best practice in my previous life, was not the way. I was expected to type up my version and then hand it to my typist assistant to re-type as News Reader Acceptable Copy. It promised to be a long 30 months ahead.

This was only relieved by an occasional diversion.

One was a Royal Hong Kong Police stop-work strike against the recently created Independent Commission Against Corruption, or ICAC. Before this major corruption syndicates were part of the fabric of life in Hong Kong. Some say it had a purpose too, as the police turned a blind eye to the gambling syndicates and low level crime to augment their meagre pay, but could also call on criminal groups, known as Triads, in the event of something more serious to help locate those responsible. The status quo was working reasonably well but the ICAC remit was draconian and by 1977 the cops had had enough. In a major demonstration against the ICAC headquarters on Hong Kong Island, rioting broke out. I was on duty in Broadcast Drive watching as army trucks arrived into the closed circuit and as each moved around the drive armed Gurkha soldiers from the resident garrison battalion jumped into the roadway, took up station every few yards and stood, automatic rifles at ready and regulation kukri fighting knives strapped to their waists, at stiff attention. We of course were aware of the disturbance and I rang Denise at our apartment to warn her to stay home in case she planned a shopping trip into Hong Kong Central district where the action was raging. The police action ended with the government's wise heads offering an amnesty for past police indiscretions.

But what followed summed up for me the general station ineptness. The governor, Sir Murray Maclehose was certainly the most qualified civil servant in the colony. He made a tape at his Government House mansion to be delivered to the studio and broadcast to calm the populace.

It ran on air for several minutes before someone woke up to the fact that it had not been cued up on arrival and was running backwards, totally incoherent. I just figured it was par for the course. As the ICAC continued its work, it's probably fair to say that the popular acceptance of bribery as a component of social life gradually faded away during the Maclehose years.

Disenchantment was a byword of my service particularly working 12 hour shifts, the first from 8am to 8pm, and the immediate next from 8pm to 8am, followed by a day asleep and then one clear day off. Apparently the idea of the all-nighter was that a 'programme officer' – for such was my designation – was always on communication duty in the colony in case disaster happened. Like perhaps an invasion from China under the then communist leader Mao Tse Tung.

In fact that worthy died while I was working in September 1976 and the world media pretty much reported the event from Hong Kong at a time following China's cultural revolution when few had access to the mainland. For government radio, the death was of course noted in bulletins while Hong Kong's Chinese population was pretty staunchly of nationalist bent. I don't think a lot of tears were shed, especially by the large number of refugees who had made it across the border to Hong Kong's fabled Golden Mountain. If they managed to reach the urban area of Kowloon it was a home run and the right to stay. If not, they were sent home to China and an uncertain future.

On the plus side for us though, Hong Kong was a vibrant city with an accompanying social life. I caught up here with Michael O'Neill who left New Plymouth with we four hopefuls in 1965. After a newspaper job in Newcastle in Australia he had made his way to Hong Kong as well. He was involved in setting up a news magazine venture, *Asiaweek*, which in later years grew into a major Asian player.

On a contract with a 25 percent gratuity payable on completion, I paid a quarter of my salary in rent, food was cheap and an otherwise disposable income meant much exotic dining out and expatriate beach and boating picnics as well as house parties most weekends. Sadly, onerous work shift conditions for me meant many social invitations were missed. But for all the available frivolity a time of much more responsibility hit when my son Shaun was born a month after the Chinese leader departed this earth.

The details are another more personal story. Suffice to say, his premature entry into this world meant the freedom of choice I had lived was now over. It was initially beset with problems stemming from his diaphragmatic hernia and perhaps the only blessing of government service was that medical care was free. It happened that the Reader of Paediatric Surgery at the University of Hong Kong, Dr Paul Yue, was called in to operate hours after the birth. For the long story, Shaun has since provided me with two strapping grandsons while achieving great success both as a chef and a top-level graphic designer and photographer.

But for many months after the birth it was a time of

great strain alleviated only by having the wherewithal to employ an excellent Filipina house maid and child helper who arrived courtesy of neighbours who were leaving Hong Kong for New Zealand – thus we knew the lass already.

Life in government employ went on and its impersonal face continued my jaundiced view of HMG's regime. A classic example of this was during one of the not infrequent typhoon alerts issued by the Royal Observatory under their signals 1, 3, 8, 9, 10 with 1 signifying a storm 800 miles from the colony and so on, with the latter being a direct hit. Usually at signal 3 everyone went home or hid at their favourite club bar for the duration. That is except for the news staff on duty. One late scale alert accompanied by torrential rain, I was being driven to work by Denise when traffic came to a standstill on Pokfulam Road into Central District. I decided to get out and walk past whatever was holding up traffic and grab a taxi. I soon came upon a slip from the hill above the road. Several local Chinese policemen were checking the scene and I stopped to ask if there were any casualties. As I did, the bush covered hill opposite began to shake, as though a giant was on a rampage. The cop I was talking to grabbed my arm and hustled me onto the footpath as a torrent of hillside surged down and across the road. A line of empty double decker buses stalled by the original slip were picked up and pushed to the opposite deep gutter abutting the footpath and tipped at 40 degrees so the roofs hit the tall buildings lining the road. The roar was disconcerting and I found myself propelled by the cop, as panicked as I was, down the tunnel formed by the leaning vehicles.

We, and others like us, emerged unscathed. I stopped at a coffee shop with a telephone to call the office with the news of a blocked major artery. The reaction I got was one of disinterest. "Yes, this happens in typhoons, but you are bloody late for work." Yes, my attitude from then on probably had a red pen scrawling through my contract file.

There was a tragic example too of the Hong Long indifference to events when, as the only male at home during the day in the complex as I was on shift work, a death occurred. From our third floor balcony, I saw two women on the ground floor running in apparent panic around the side of the building. I crossed the large lounge and looked out a rear window to see a young woman lying on the first floor wire mesh horizontal screen designed to catch a falling item like a pot plant or a child's toy from higher windows. She lay still, blood flowing from her head onto the paved courtyard below. I went down the back stairs and climbed onto the wire covering, but it was clear she was dead, her head serrated into the wire cobweb. Looking up, I saw a wide open window on the 16th floor. I called up the two levels to our kitchen window and asked Denise to throw down a sheet while I waited for the police, alerted by one of the women who had caused me to find the body.

When several Chinese policemen arrived, they simply established the death, arranged for the body removal by ambulance and that was it. There was not a question in my direction about what had happened. I imagined the police report: "Servant fell out window and was dead. No further action needed." As a footnote, the sheet I had used to cover the woman, who was a Filapina servant, was from a wedding present linen set and unused, But our Filipina girl refused to handle it again, for 'ghost' reasons, so it was disposed of.

There was the odd relieving moment in life though. A friendship with expat police superintendent Bill Duncanson, who headed the paramilitary armed offender squad, saw me invited to relive my youthful marksmanship days in New Zealand on their combat course. The colony had an auxiliary police component of otherwise bored civil servants who acted as territorials to make up numbers as needed for events, crowd control and the like, so for a few hours I was temporarily inducted as such, bad leg ignored, to satisfy an official form. The day's training for the specialist anti-terror squad involved Sten machine guns and automatic AR 15 rifles, some being fired from city environment concrete building mockups which had devastating concussion effects resounding in the enclosed space. The next time you watch a TV show with cops decimating bad guys in a closed environment, don't believe it without extensive ear protection being apparent. However, Bill decided if push came to shove, he would include me in a real scenario due to my marksmanship skills.

Our social group outside of work colleagues consisted of a wide selection of expats, from the police hierarchy like Bill, to local business entrepreneurs, engineers, shipping managers and Cathay Pacific airline crew, a couple of garrison army blokes and all their wives. One mining engineer was employed on the construction of a massive fresh water reservoir in the New Territories, essential infrastructure at a time when it was not unknown for China to switch off the pumps supplying water from across the border. There was a massive seawater desalination plant in operation on Kowloon, with local legend blaming it for a harsh local beer brand.

The High Island Reservoir was a massive undertaking and much of its area was carved out by explosives overseen by Ken, our Australian engineer mate. The project linked two main dams from the mainland to High Island that was filled with water from a massive land catchment on completion.

With our engineer in charge, our social group had a picnic and barbecue for about 30 of us on the day before the inundation was due to begin, so we gathered at the floor of the dam for the occasion. It was there we discovered a wrecked sampan containing a pile of ancient pottery pieces that must have been many years old considering the huge depth involved with the sea floor pumped dry. This was to have ramifications for me much later on. Suffice to say, we few can claim to be the last visitors to ground zero that now holds some 300 million cubic metres of water, and when at full capacity, the surface stands 61.5 metres above sea level.

On the work front, I did have one assignment of interest when I was sent off to do a feature story. This involved a ferry-ride to a corner of the New Territories where ships from around the world ended their last voyage and were broken up for recycling into the one main essential for the construction of high-rise Hong Kong, rebar – or simply reinforcing steel. I watched in fascination as tons of steel plate was sent into furnaces to emerge molten and then channelled into narrow moulds to emerge steaming and black in long lengths of building reinforcement.

I recorded an interview with an expat overseer, but I did not use his observation that it had been known for some construction companies to use free and available seawater in their concrete mix with disastrous end results in some cases. Less said the better where HMG was involved eh?

My last clash with HMG involved an age old media lurk, known as 'the rat', whereby one could earn a bit of beer money sending a story to another media outlet. I had a deal to send 30 second news voice reports by telephone to New Zealand's state radio as well as Radio 4IP in Australia and did so, earning a nest egg on each occasion. But that earned me a major rap in a cease and desist memo from HMG because, silly me, I used my own name apart from my voice, figuring who, in Hong Kong, would know 6,000 miles away. Yes, I had forgotten that HMG had a consul in Auckland with not much to do between cocktails and job interviews but listen to the radio.

One incident that always jumps into mind whenever a certain singer's recordings appears on air is a narrow escape from professional disaster at Radio Hong Kong. I was driving a rather lovely and rare MGB Jubilee Edition, in midnight blue with gold highlights marking the 50 years since the marque appeared. I'd bought it from a Hong Kong policeman 'leaving town in a rush' after the ICAC episode and I would drive reluctantly to work on a night shift often playing Elvis Presley tapes on the tape deck. *'In The Ghetto'* was one track of choice reflecting my mood.

On this occasion, with my shift ending at 8 am after the morning news bulletin was handed off to the announcer, I decided to sneak away at 7.30, ready for breakfast and a good sleep. But I had forgotten my meal thermos still on my desk so stopped my MGB at the station gate and popped back upstairs to find my frantic Indian typist and an agitated Chinese channel staff.

Elvis Presley died of a heart attack at the age of 42 on August 16th 1977 at his Graceland home in Memphis, Tennessee and that bulletin was spilling from the teleprinter as I entered the newsroom. I made the addition for the typist to finish and an office messenger to run down two flights of stairs in time to make the lead to the news at 8. I would have probably been carpeted or worse if I had not stepped back to the newsroom and I had a few nervous beers for breakfast when I got home to help me get off to sleep, lulled by a rumbling air conditioner while Denise went off to coffee mornings or shopping and visiting. Shifts were not conducive to companionship.

Finally though, freedom beckoned and after a brief three month extension to my contract, we were finally thankful to head back to New Zealand and what we felt was a better long-term care regime as Shaun reached his second birthday. But there's a footnote which adds to the overall HMG reflection. Just before my last day at work, more than two years since they were ordered by the station, I was handed 500 official RTHK embossed business cards, in English and Chinese characters, bearing the official translation of my name. This was *Kan Pok Lim*. It translates as *"man of great erudition"* – Well that accolade was too bloody late in coming.

However, a benefit involved in the job was that the return passage home was easily variable within the government fare allowance and we were able to make a pleasant excursion through Asia on the way back to Auckland.

Another Kiwi expat I knew well from my Auckland days, the late Simon Halley, ran a travel trade magazine and he pulled some strings which got us free hotels en route. From Kong Kong's Kai Tak (today it is a park and a housing estate) we flew the 'Orange' safe air route over the Vietnam war zone and stayed at the Bangkok Oriental on the edge of the Mekong River and its luxurious Somerset Maugham Wing. On to Singapore and a luxury motel, then to Bali and an hotel and then a beachside bungalow and swimming pool for a week. Our visit was made pleasant too because Shaun was a blond and blue eyed munchkin who captivated the local Indonesian women who sold souvenirs along the beach, swapping fabulous carvings for a simple T shirt, or as Denise found, items of clean new underwear. We sunbathed and swam as Shaun was safely entertained nearby by his admirers.

But all things come to an end and paradise found soon meant the airport at Den Pasar again. We had a flight delay, reaching Sydney too late for our next scheduled flight and wielding a credit card, ran to get business class seats that was all that was left on a 747 across the Tasman.

CHAPTER TWELVE

AUCKLAND WAS A breath of literal fresh air, but it also turned somewhat sour when Hong Kong had a sting in its tail, occasioned by an intensive customs search when our personal goods shipment arrived by sea. A taciturn customs inspector gave us the third degree and searched our personal and household possessions with a thoroughness that bemused us. When he found a box of grey pieces of hardened material his eyes lit up and a deep conversation was held with his attending staff. It took some time before I convinced him that these were very old Chinese pottery fragments kept as a souvenir from High Island. In the end, he left empty-handed while we had to repack from the disorder he left behind. It was while doing a post-mortem on this experience that we heard that a lady ex Hauraki colleague who had stayed as a house guest in our government flat, had later been caught posting some dope through the mail from London to a friend in New Zealand. So obviously we had become 'persons of interest' by virtue of having had contact with the lady overseas.

That little drama over we still made a little money flogging some cheap Hong Kong goods to friends and family as organised and in ensuing weeks we bought a house and resettled ourselves to a quieter existence. On the job front, an extraordinary Kiwi entrepreneur Gordon Dryden was a pioneer of local talkback radio, who I remembered from 1973 when he began hosting a daily talk show called Powerline on Auckland's Radio 1, one of a plethora of private radio outlets that jumped on the Hauraki bandwagon around the country. My old Hauraki comrade Tom Clarke was running news for the new Radio Avon in Christchurch. In 1979 Gordon opened Radio Pacific, New Zealand's first all-newstalk station, and I landed the job as his Chief Reporter on a large news staff reminiscent of Hauraki days.

Gordon was not backward in coming forward with plans and ideas and he figured Radio Pacific should know something about its namesake geographic region. With my wife and son in tow, I was soon flying off to Tonga, Samoa and Fiji on a 10-day familiarisation jaunt as the station was set up in a new building in South Auckland. In fact the trip was a very pleasant 'junket' with little value to ensue as far as station programming went, but it helped establish a rapport with the South Auckland community which had a major Pacific Island populace.

I was soon back in the thick of news gathering and it was great to again be working with an enthusiastic staff of journalists and the other station staff of technicians, advertising, office and on-air people. With its news talk format, we played a major part of programming with Dryden and other personalities leading public discussion on current events across the news spectrum.

In July of that first year on Pacific, I once again picked up on New Zealand's now infamous Crewe murder case that I had first covered while I was with Radio Hauraki. Arthur Allan Thomas was granted a royal pardon after being wrongfully convicted of the murders of Harvey and Jeannette Crewe in June 1970. Thomas was married and farming at Pukekawa south of Auckland when the Crewe's were shot dead by bullets from a .22 rifle In their farmhouse and their bodies dumped in the nearby Waikato River.

After nine years of trials and appeals, it was finally revealed that the crucial evidence against him had been faked, Thomas was awarded compensation for his years in prison and loss of earnings. The pardon was issued by then Prime Minister Robert Muldoon and soon afterwards a Royal Commission of Inquiry confirmed that a cartridge case in the Crewe's garden – said to have come from a rifle belonging to Thomas – was planted at the scene by a detective. However no-one was ever charged with a crime in so doing. Much of the work in clearing Thomas was done by top kiwi journalist and editor, Pat Booth, a close Dryden confidant.

The movie *Beyond Reasonable Doubt* told the Crewe murders story and aftermath and was a box office success in New Zealand such was the public awareness of the case and it in turn stemmed from a book by British author David Yallop.

In Radio Pacific's case, Dryden led the way He flew by helicopter to meet Thomas on his release and scooped the national media in so doing. As a news operation we were underway where Hauraki had left off as its news commitment dwindled in the face of competition in the music station genre, relying more and more on syndicated and shared news. I had something of a mantra to the entire Pacific staff that we "are all news gatherers, from Dryden on down to the office cleaner. If you see or hear of something happening, tell the newsroom."

But in the way of news stories, they come out of the blue when least expected and such was the case on November 28th 1979 when my telephone rang just as I was preparing for an early bed prior to a breakfast news shift at 6am. "It's your office," said Denise, handing me the phone. An evening staff reporter stumbled over the words. "There's a plane missing, that Air New Zealand Antarctic flight. What do we need to do?" I established that all hands were at the pump in the office and that further news was coming from Air New Zealand headquarters, just minutes from my house near the Auckland city centre. I hurriedly dressed and headed in to take up position there and quickly caught up with the situation unfolding.

The DC10 with 257 passengers and crew was on a much publicised scenic flight to overfly the Antarctic iceland and had not been heard from for several hours so in my own mind a plane missing in Antarctica was likely not coming back. This was confirmed just an hour after I got the call, when airline boss Morry Davis announced that flight TE901 was believed lost because, by then, it had exhausted its fuel supply.

I made a phone report live to air as around me Air New Zealand staff who had been waiting at work for news burst into tears and hugged each other in despair. As I reported Davis' confirmation a young woman secretary maybe saw me as a calm male figure and reached up and held me, crying into my shoulder. Mid-report, my throat caught and tears welled in my own eyes. I signed off with a raspy ad lib about "an intense and emotional scene is unfolding here... more details when I can." Human touch can do that sometimes, and while a professional lapse, I guess it adds 'colour' to the message on radio.

At some later point, the passenger and crew list was released and I was back at the station to hear a broadcast in the dawn as announcer David Beatson read those names, one by one, over the air. Staff, my self included, joined our listeners across Auckland in sudden shock as names were recognised. It was later obvious that many thousands of listeners had lost family members, friends, or acquaintances.

What was an intensive search by US air units in Antarctica and a Royal New Zealand Airforce Orion had culminated at 1.25am on November 29th 1979, when charred wreckage was formally identified as the remains of flight TE901 by an American helicopter. There was simply a blackened smear of wreckage strewn across the 3,800 metre Mt. Erebus, on Ross Island to mark New Zealand's worst air disaster. An official crash website records that: 'with the wreckage located, the priorities became the search for survivors and the two flight recorders. The first men at the crash site on the morning of November 29th 1979 were experienced New Zealand mountaineers. They were confronted by a horrific scene scattered with personal possessions and human remains. The men established a 'base camp' for the recovery operation: eight polar tents, sleeping bags and food for 20 people for a few days. That evening they were joined by a recovery team from New Zealand, but bad weather hampered search efforts for the next two days'.

Our news bulletins recorded the lengthy recovery operation with repatriation flights by RNZAF Hercules transports to a make-shift morgue at the Whenuapai base in west Auckland. There were harrowing details of identification teams and the ongoing trauma of the job. For instance, one victim identification came down to a key from a rental car found at the airport car park, embedded in flesh from the crash. In a world of tragic events, Erebus stands permanently etched in my, and the national recollective. But when, so to speak, the dust cleared, Air New Zealand pointed to pilot error but public reaction was sufficient to prompt a Royal Commission of Inquiry by Justice Peter Mahon QC, who decided the cause was a correction made to the electronic coordinates of the flight path the night before the tragedy and failure to tell the flight crew of the change, So instead of being directed down McMurdo Sound as the crew was instructed, it was heading straight into Erebus in white out conditions. Air New Zealand was cited for "an orchestrated litany of lies" and this led to a management exodus.

CHAPTER THIRTEEN

ON THE HOME front things were less than good, as the legendary seven year itch took hold in the relationship. Perhaps it was serendipity that an offer came up from the U.S. State Department for a familiarisation junket to the American sunbelt states, from Los Angeles through to Florida. I found myself selected with five other Kiwi journalists on a DC10 flight and a couple of weeks of escorted touring. My companions included acquaintance and peer Bruce Scott as well as four other senior blokes on a pre-retirement freebie. A light plane flight into the Grand Canyon was a heart-stopping experience as our Cessna Caravan swooped mere feet above the canyon rim to seemingly launch into space as the canyon fell away below. And an indication of a markedly different attitude I found with many Americans I met was on the return flight over the Arizona desert, the pilot banked sharply and indicated something below. It was another light plane in a crumpled heap. There were people standing around on the ground and our pilot simply said. "Been a fender bender down there. All got out," obviously monitoring radio traffic in his headphones. He was laid back as though we had seen a car with a dent in it.

Another 'laid back' experience was while traversing the boardwalk at Santa Monica Beach in LA when I head the yell "Hey Crip" as I limped along in characteristic gait. Nonplussed, I ignored what I considered ignorance but it was repeated more loudly.

I looked for the source and saw a group of young men who waved me over."Hey, come have a brew," I limped over, was handed a Budweiser can, and said caller was in a wheelchair and had no legs or hands. "Vietnam, a mine," he said sipping beer through a tube. I stayed for a quick chat before I had to catch up to my tour colleagues.

Other highlights with the US State Department picking up the tab included a visit to the bowels of the giant Hoover Dam generating room, the New Orleans Jazz and Heritage Festival and Mardi Gras and a tour of Cape Canaveral, up close and personal with giant Atlas rockets and space shuttles. But also of note was being mugged for my cash in late night New Orleans and the sight of an elderly homeless couple snuggled into the cold shelter of a ground floor bay window of the brightly lit Marriott Hotel. America was certainly a land of contrasts. But the predominant experience of the United States trip was a captain's announcement on a flight from New Orleans to Dallas, Fort Worth Somewhere 30,000 feet over Texas, from the flight deck: "Ladies and gentlemen, I have some distressing news". Now that is not what a planeload of passengers wants to hear – ever. There was a shocked silence of several long seconds then the southern drawl continued as a number of choked gasps were expelled and hands clutched at armrests. "As I said, ladies and gentleman, awful news." More dead air and a feeling of panic before: "On a monitored broadcast here in the cockpit, his Holiness the Pope has been shot." There was a muted cheer in the cabin.

As history records, on May 13th 1981 in St. Peter's

Square in Vatican City, Pope John Paul II was shot and wounded by Mehmet Ali Ağca. Obviously our pilot was one of the faithful but his on-the-job job diplomatic skills needed a refresher course.

It was soon time to fly back across the Pacific with a last stop in Hawaii and a visit to Pearl Harbour's sunken USS Arizona and back at the station time followed with all the stuff of news, political happenings, union hassles and births, deaths and marriages. But then sport suddenly became a war zone. In winter and spring of 1981, New Zealanders were launched into a polarising confrontation in a massive series of civil disturbances all stemming from the game of rugby.

At issue was the South African Springbok's tour of the country and tests against the iconic All Blacks national team as well as provincial matches. It was a white-only South African side under the country's 'apartheid' strict division of white and black races.

Subsequent official records say that more than 150,000 people took part in over 200 demonstrations in 28 centres, and 1,500 were charged with offences stemming from protests pretty much organised by HART for Halt All Racist Tours.

The Springboks arrived in provincial Gisborne on July 19th and we watched from afar in our South Auckland studios as civil conflict broke out on the part of HART inspired opponents of apartheid and supporters of the game who believed politics and sport were separate deals altogether and the game must go on. In the opening game in Poverty Bay, the stage was set for street disturbances on a national scale.

The police had long been alerted to the possibility of civil action in the lead up to the tour and despite government assurances that the rank and file could handle any problem, the cops disagreed and formed The Red Squad, a cadre of tough riot control-trained staff that became a flash point in the tour ahead as they confronted demonstrators in a sometimes over zealous manner, with long batons, shields and body armour.

At Pacific, executive staff held an editorial planning session and I found myself on my way to Hamilton with a brief to cover the 'political' story, while top sports newsman, the late Mike Parkinson, would cover the rugby action for the next scheduled game. In my case that all turned a bit nasty.

Rugby Park in Hamilton was packed and more than 500 cops were on duty as around 5,000 demonstrators, many clad in motorcycle helmets and other protective gear, anticipated a day of action. And action there was as before the game could start the mob tore down the high perimeter fencing and flooded the footy field with protesters. Police moved in and there was a tense standoff between the invaders and the rugby supporters with the odd fight erupting in the melee.

With other media, I watched all this happening from some four metres in the air on a truck bed with a scissor effect hydraulic hoist that gave us a level platform and vantage point. It had a banner designating us as media for the world to see. We then had a report that a light plane was inbound to the field and with that the police told the local ruby union the match was cancelled due to the danger of a potential suicide mission. Now it was the turn of game supporters to get out of hand and they began attacking protesters with fists, boots, cans and bottles. Then the cry went up "Get the bloody media, it's all their fault", and a section began fighting their way to where we perched at a dangerous height. In fact, we had a police detective disguised among us in our vantage point, with radio contact with his colleagues. Thank God for that because we were in imminent danger of the truck being toppled by a hundred or so large and very angry rugby fans. He managed to call in a squad of police who defended us as the hoist was lowered, then stood by as the thwarted assault moved to the streets adjacent, continuing some brutal assaults and property damage into the centre of the town. It was a demonstration of hysterical mob frenzy I had never seen in New Zealand. Of course, with the concentration of media, violent images were relayed around the world. That night in the lounge bar of a city hotel, many beers went down as we compared notes, with the infamous Red Squad cops doing a haka to boost morale. A reporting phone call to Radio Pacific led to a request that I carry on with the tour and the next stop, my old hometown, New Plymouth.

In fact, due to a HART change in tactics, this third game of tour was remarkably peaceful simply because the police outnumbered the protestors. This was due in no small measure to the fact that HART supremo John Minto and his cohorts changed strategy and were organising major demos in Auckland and outside parliament in Wellington for better media exposure. We were actually able to watch a good game of rugby pretty much undisturbed bar a few placard wavers outside the showgrounds. Then it was on to Wanganui and a similar situation where just 100 or so demonstrators had little effect beyond chanting and placard waving and the Springboks won 45-9.

Palmerston North was the next game scheduled against Manawatu and after the clashes in Wellington where police were less than gentle outside Parliament, things looked grim with some 5,000 HART adherents gathering with protective headgear, clothing and cricket pads and armed with bats, hockey sticks and other makeshift weapons.

The game was at the town show-grounds which had been ringed like a fortress with dumpsters full of sand where the Red Squad stood in ranks. Rumour had it that about 1,000 police officers were in Palmerston North and ready for action.

Well the 5,000 marchers neared the police lines and for some stupid reason I thought I should go for sound effects to spice up my voice reports and record the massed chants of "Amandla Soweto" and "Don't scrum with scum" as the mob stepped in unison towards the rows of armed cops. I stood just in front and slightly to the side of the converging forces, microphone raised. But suddenly I was hoisted off my feet and carried away a couple of yards and set down in a small building entrance doorway. My large and smiling captor in jeans and a leather jacket just chuckled. "Senior segeant xxxx," he said. "that was no place for you." As I watched, the Red Squad stepped forward in unison, batons raised and meaning business. "They wouldn't have stopped for you mate," said my helpful cop.

As it was the demonstration leaders, bruised from Wellington apparently, had second thoughts, saw the physical clash was coming and turned away to lead the march back into the city, The Manawatu game was played.

The next stop was Wellington and on reporting back to base I suggested staff in the capital could take up the chase. Time for me to head home. My last tour experience was that night at the motel we stayed in along with a number of South African media men. In the house bar late that night, with connivance from a motel staffer, we rigged up my recording of protest chants and stuck a stereo speaker outside the bar into the motel forecourt at high volume. Lights flashed on, doors opened and sleepy 'yarpy' newsmen gathered on their balconies. Very naughty and perhaps a good thing that I headed out early for the drive back to Auckland. The tour went on to end in much more major drama in Auckland with flour bombs hurled from a light aircraft into the rugby game at Eden Park, all on live world-wide television.

CHAPTER FOURTEEN

BACK HOME MATTERS rather came to a head and there was a splitting of the marriage. I was convinced that a continually argumentative couple was no way to care for a then rising five-year-old and decided to take one combatant out of the equation. If there is one certainty in a journalism career involving draconian shifts and extended hours, it is that a personal social life in a normal sense goes out the door. It may be as simple as ships passing in the night but it is a heavy burden and I do believe it's an extraordinary union that will survive intact in a life of constantly evolving shift work.

I'd befriended a fellow journalist based in Los Angeles, Jim Thompson, who served the national Mutual Radio Network and I'd set him up as Radio Pacific's American correspondent when he visited New Zealand. So we talked regularly and always thought we would compliment each other's skills. To cut another long story short, I flew back over the Pacific but soon found suburban Glendale and the American way good to visit, but less so to live with.

I might have been thought as a man of the world, but Jim organised a night tour of LA in the form of a police ride-along. I was delivered by an associate of his, Chuck, a nightbeat reporter, to the downtown LAPD headquarters around 10pm one night and taken under the wing of a police sergeant. His duty involved responding as a controlling authority to any incident requiring assistance and to organise resources on the ground accordingly. Before setting off, the sergeant pointed to a key attached to his ignition and then at a gleaming shotgun locked in a horizontal rack across the front bench seat of his patrol car. "That key unlocks that weapon if we have a problem and I need help," was all he said. What followed saw us attend a drive-by gang shooting in East LA where a young woman was nursing a bullet wound in her leg. We stayed until an ambulance and paramedics took over. There was an attempted suicide from a tall crane on a five storey building site eventually talked down by a woman police negotiator. Another call to a missing person report found an elderly woman in a dilapidated bungalow surrounded by rubbish and cats where my escort deduced the missing husband had actually died a year before. We stopped to check on two young women on a darkened street and my cop suggested they "go to work where there's some light, ladies". Our tour ended by following the spotlight of a low flying police helicopter trying to locate a hit and run driver. But we peeled off and were soon back at headquarters, where, over coffee, the assignment was handed over to a relief sergeant who resumed the patrol. Chuck picked me up and on the way back to Glendale we stopped at a drive-in diner. It was busy with late-night denizens. Chuck simply turned up the volume of his police radio scanner and most of them melted away into the night as he bought us a taco supper for the continuing ride home. So it might have been exciting, but in fact, LA seemed a little tawdry and perhaps overwhelming.

Now Asia was a different story, with many good

friends and contacts from my stint with HMG, and after a yarn with Jim in my vulnerable 'just out of a broken marriage cloud' I flew back to Hong Kong via Tokyo and in a week I was hired as assistant managing editor for Television Broadcasts, TVB, owned by Chinese movie magnate Run Run Shaw, on the commercial English language Pearl Channel.

The working hours were tailor made for a recently single Hong Kong expatriate with a midday start and a 7pm finish. There was a main evening bulletin at 6pm, and a 'late' broadcast at 9pm, which in effect was just a partial recording of the earlier event.

Shortly after I had set up in a shared flat in Broadcast Drive I was on a visit to a Wanchai night club when I had a sudden flashback to my earlier stay in Hong Kong. My wife and I had befriended our daily newspaper delivery 'boy', a Sonny Lam, aged about 24 and his young wife. It was an unusual link and I put it down to our Kiwi equality of manner. At some stage it became apparent that newspaper delivery to the 300 or so apartments in the complex was a 'franchise' with substantial money involved, no doubt with a touch of the underworld about it. Now I was having a quiet beer when an arm reached from behind me to pull a new frosted bottle from a bench top icebox below the bar level and place it before me. I turned to find Sonny, the newspaper 'boy'. The lady manager behind the bar gave him a nod and a smile and made no attempt at seeking payment. Sonny gave me a friendly thump on the back, welcomed me back, and helped himself to another beer. It was soon obvious that his days of newspapers were long past, and it transpired in fact that he was a triad office bearer with the local Sun Yee On chapter. In other words, a very good local to have on your side. I'm pretty certain, while we crossed paths on many similar occasions, always with a new beer being produced, that I had benevolent eyes on me for the rest of my stay in the shadows of the night in the colony.

It was more amply demonstrated when Mr Lee, the owner of several Hong Kong night spots suddenly called me out of a group, and bade me join him for a late night dinner at a swept-up local restaurant. When I looked puzzled at the honour he added "for happy birthday to you." It was within days of that date, and I realised why when I found Sonny in a group of 'prominent' locals at the large round table. He had kept tabs since our early association. Mr Lee, it transpired, had just become a father with his current Second Wife, or mistress and for some reason he wanted a nice "name from New Zealand not England name." There was a peculiarity of the British colony, due in some part to disillusioned English teachers who christened uncooperative Chinese kids with names like 'Cowboy' Wong and 'Hitler' Chow, that then became official names of record. I even knew of a lass called Supermarket Chan, whose labourer father copied it from a shop sign and I assume Mr Lee did not approve. Inspiration struck me with 'Manu' the Maori for bird, which delighted him. "Ah, so. Manu! This will be. Manu Lee", and another round table toast was called for.

Most early evenings found yours truly in the RTHK bar, a watering hole run by the estimable Mr Wong who probably paid a peppercorn rental to service the station staff, as well as sundry other expatriates living in nearby government flats. These included police inspectors, the odd air traffic controller from nearby Kai Tak airport or other civil servants.

It was in the RTHK bar that met another lifelong friend-to-be in Sidney Anthony Baynes, 'Tony' to all, who was at that time head of English language radio after a career with the BBC in the UK. We cemented that friendship within a few weeks after he roped me into a live broadcast operation covering the start of the annual South China Sea yacht race from Hong Kong's Victoria Harbour to Manila in the Philippines.

I was aboard the local charter vessel Ji Fung together with a TVB crew as a double involvement. With the virtual amphitheatre created by the backdrop of Hong Kong Island and its towering architecture stepping up the steep hills to the Peak mansions, the start on the blue harbour was a sight made for television, and the live radio broadcast with smoothly executed crosses to me and another reporting station all compered by Tony in a command vessel, provided a real time commentary to possibly a million watchers. The race included serious sailing competitors and a large social flotilla, the shellback racers.

With representation from many of the 'hongs' the great trading houses of Asia like Jardine Matheson, the Hong Kong Shanghai Bank and others, the shellback was all about luxury at sea for some, pressed duck and caviar and fine wines of course. As the yachts jilled about before making for the start line out of the harbour my TV crew managed to catch some footage which fascinated our viewers that evening, as a 'hong' yacht cruised alongside our vessel with the eight man expatriate crew lined up at attention along the rail. At their feet, with legs dangling over the side, were eight life-size inflatable plastic sex dolls. I used the clip in the evening bulletin. TVB's controller of news Ray Wong looked sideways at me the next day, but made no comment.

Ray's humour however did not encompass another European form of expression when British comic supremo Spike Milligan visited TVB, presumably for a Chinese Channel entertainment segment of some sort. However, he found his way into the English news studio prior to the newsreader getting the red light to broadcast. The next thing we saw as the news at 6 broadcast began was Milligan standing behind the desk, waving and grinning demonically with one arm with his spare hand holding a banana, end-on, to his ear. At the first 'sound on tape' video segment, he was escorted out of the studio. A post mortem led to a major row blaming the newsreader – all his fault in the eyes of the management. However, the worthy newsreader left to become, I believe Hong Kong's co-ordinator of an international charity "Save the Something" and was no doubt quite happy with corporate salary, perks in accommodation and such.

But for neighbouring RTHK, what was most striking about Tony Baynes tenure was the infusion of expertise and flair into the antediluvian radio that had been my job experience of a few years earlier. Mr Baynes, as of course he was always referred to by the Chinese portion of his staff, knew radio from his early days running his own show in the British 'geordie' provinces, and that live yachting broadcast marked a new beginning. Before long the station was involved in myriad community activities. Tony had in fact arrived to the disorder that I had found and left and he remembers his own confusing experience:

> Hong Kong was a blow to the senses, in November 1979 which began as the flight banked sharply to starboard across Chequerboard Hill, so named because of the red and white squares painted thereon to mark final approach into the old Kai Tak airport in Kowloon, Gow Lung literally, the 'nine dragons', the hills which hid the vast expanse of the Chinese mainland from the then British Crown Colony.
>
> I was supposed to be met at the Kai Tak terminal by a representative of Radio Television Hong Kong, the government radio and fledgling TV programme maker that had offered me employment. Of course, there had been a stuff up, but I managed to hitch a ride with a fellow passenger who took me to what was then the Foreign Correspondents Club on Hong Kong island, colloquially Hong Kong side. It was in Sutherland House, a colonial era structure, on the 15th floor. I used the toilet overlooking Hong Kong Harbour, made iconic by author John Le Carré, in his book The Honourable Schoolboy. He described it as the toilet with the world's best view. He was right!

The snafu over my meeting was resolved, and I soon found myself ensconced in bachelor accommodation at Ho Man Tin, on Kowloon side and starting work at RTHK.

And that was an eye-opener. As the newbie, and single, I found myself on the shit shifts, with little cooperation from fellow workers who somehow felt threatened by my BBC background. RTHK had evolved from a polyglot public service pool of 'talent'. Some people had little background in the jobs they held. I well remember December 25th 1979. I was live from early morning till early afternoon, the Christmas Day shift. At about noon, I ventured downstairs to the lower ground floor to the so-called staff canteen. It was something out of a street stall, with kitchen grime holding it together. Unable to face this, and then a staff toilet that resembled a squatters hut facility – a previous user had squatted oriental style on the seat to perform ablutions and simply missed – I wondered what the hell I had let myself in for.

Mildly depressed, I found my way to the RTHK bar, run by an affable gentleman called Mr Wong. Here at least was a cold beer. It was not long though before a kind invitation to dinner and an assimilation into the company of friendlier souls, that my spirits rose and I got to grips with a city that was a byword for excitement.

Soon I had my own Amah, a lovely lady dressed in a traditional black and white maid's uniform. She had her own quarters at the back of the house and looked after me mightily. She had placed a bowl with a goldfish at the bottom of some steps that led to my bedroom. "Good joss," she'd say. Apparently the bad spirits would not pass a lucky goldfish on their way to my bedroom so I was protected.

However, a year passed and things began to change. Inflation! ...and so I set about making economies. The amah, together with the comprador, a driver/butler/handyman/manager, ran the accounts. "What's this?" I said pointing to a line of Chinese script with a largish number at the end... "For goal fish," explained the compradore. "It must be a very valuable goldfish," I replied. "No, no, no," he continued "for 365 goal fish. Every night you take one whiskey too many... every night you put whiskey in goal fish bowl. Every morning before you wake I put new goal fish!"

It sounded very fishy to me... but that said, that worthy redeemed himself very quickly. The fish lived much longer.

Another memory is of the pop band Police playing in Hong Kong. It was the night of the BBC's Top of the Pops awards programme and Police were to receive a gold disc award via a live TV link with London. I was the liaison producer and before the event the band came on my morning show. Sting, a fellow Geordie, was desperate for a bottle of Newcastle

Brown Ale, the one thing that he missed as he travelled the world. "No problem," I said and within minutes I had called the compradore who quickly sourced a couple of cases of the required ale which was available in the British colony drinking establishments. That afternoon, I took Sting and Stewart Copeland on a junk trip around Aberdeen Harbour. They loved it... the trip and the Brown Ale!

A major topic of the time of course was the impending takeover of Hong Kong by China in 1997, and I did a number of interviews on the subject, one of which is entrenched in my memory. As I lived near the station, I was called in early one day to replace a host who had called in sick. News producer on duty was Scotsman Terry Nealon, who assured me all was prepared for an interview with Lord Carrington, who was in town on his way to Beijing to meet Deng Xiao Ping to discuss the Hong Kong handover to China.

At the appropriate time, we crossed to our Hong Kong studio at Sutherland House and I launched into the first pre-prepared question on my crib sheet.

"Is that a pejorative question?" replied Lord Carrington. I killed the mike and buzzed Terry in the control room. "What the bloody hell does pejorative mean?" Terry looked puzzled and, fearful of dead air, quick as a flash I reopened my mike and said "Well you clearly seem to think it is. How so?" Somehow the interview settled down and went fine. On another occasion we were expecting a visit from Sir Peter Blaker, a former diplomat, Conservative MP for Blackpool South, and a government minister.

Sir Peter was running late, and I went downstairs to the lobby to rush him to the studio. Sure enough, up came a large black limo and I hustled the visitor in. Alas it was too late to make the time slot so I led Sir Peter down to the Green Room and made him a coffee while the BBC World News ran its course. "Milk and sugar Sir Peter?" I said. I then began to make small talk and it was only when I referred to him a second time as Sir Peter that he pointed out that he was an orchestra conductor who'd come to record a Fine Music programme! "OUT OUT, I thought and rapidly ushered him, with coffee in hand to the recording studio before rushing back to the lobby to find the real Sir Peter Blaker. All part of a day's work.

Charity work was a regular feature of expat life in the colony. I resurrected one project, Operation Santa Claus, which raised funds for the impoverished in a city with little or no public assistance available. Beggars were a common sight on strategic street corners. We often involved staff from the British services in these activities, team races and contests. On one occasion we were entertaining crowds at the Star Ferry terminal in Tsim Sha Tsui, in Kowloon, when the police arrived. We apparently had no permit for the gathering. Perhaps they were remembering the Star Ferry fare rise riots of some years before. However, when we explained what was happening, all was allowed to proceed.

But on my first arrival in Hong Kong what struck me most was the disorder. The government bureaucratic chaos and the stupidity. I had taken a step down and a pay increase to get the job because they couldn't bring in a senior person above their lifers. So after my first contract, by May 1981 I was promoted to Senior Programme Officer. Then things started to happen.

The previous presenters, and indeed management, did not understand that RTHK was a government-funded service based on the BBC promise to: Inform, Educate and Entertain, in that order and that we needed to talk with our listeners and understand who they were. In other words our listeners were not head-banging, rock n rollers, they were predominantly female, middle class adults, as opposed to teenagers, whose husbands were at work during the day and who listened to the radio for company.

Our listeners were part of a bigger English speaking community and we too were part of that same community and needed to circulate within it and support it in every way, So I set about getting outside and meeting our listeners at their events. We soon were involved closely in dozens of events – including of course the

Start of the China Sea Race.

Tony's gift of communicating set a new standard.

CHAPTER FIFTEEN

THE NEXT DECADE I was to spend in the British colony was one of an ever evolving political news story on the international stage. It was apparent that the British lease of the mainland enclave of Kowloon and the New Territories was going to run out and serious talks were underway between Prime Minister Margaret Thatcher's government and China on the premise that capitalism would still hold sway for 50 years after China took the ropes overall.

There was a dramatic focus on the talks in 1982 when local Chinese newspapers commented that in discussion in Beijing, Mrs Thatcher was 'beaten back to her original role as a woman' when she slipped and fell on the steps of the Great Hall of the People in front of the world's TV. The Iron Lady finally "succumbed to Chinese leader Deng Xiaoping, an opponent who was harder than steel," crowed a Beijing-backed Hong Kong newspaper.

We of course ran the nasty fall on TVB. Later many commentators felt Britain had "retreated steadily" in Sino-British negotiations and "failed to defend the best interests of the people of Hong Kong." The takeover was still over a decade away, but with the future of some six million local people in the mix, the unfolding saga was always top of mind.

In true colonial fashion HMG were expert in the time-honoured diplomatic mushroom process. Despite millions depending on the outcome of talks, keep them in the dark eating bullshit was the official attitude, as evidenced by the record of British House of Commons Hansard which I have kept that quotes Tony's interview mishap subject, Sir Peter. Blaker, as chairman of the Anglo-Hong Kong parliamentary group:

> China and the United Kingdom have a strong common interest in Hong Kong remaining prosperous and if it is to remain prosperous it must retain its traditional way of life. The prosperity of Hong Kong, so remarkably achieved, is of great advantage to the people of Hong Kong who have created for themselves under British guidance a standard of living better than that of almost any other country in Asia.
>
> It is useful that a dialogue is taking place between the members of the Executive Council and Her Majesty's Government. The issue has been debated whether it is right for Her Majesty's Government to maintain silence about the content of the negotiations. I believe it is indeed right that Her Majesty's Government should continue to regard the talks as confidential. Complicated points will be discussed in the negotiations as we get deeper into them. They will involve complex and detailed matters, and that is an added reason why the Government should continue to observe confidentiality. That is the best guarantee of success.

Then this from then Minister of State, Foreign and Commonwealth Affairs, Richard Luce:

There is an overwhelming desire on the part of the people at all levels in Hong Kong – in the villages, in the New Territories, in the urban city areas, at a humble or very senior level to see continuity of their way of life. I found that when I visited Hong Kong recently. I sense that there is an understanding of why it is important that the talks should remain confidential, as was agreed between the British and Chinese Governments originally. Looking over our history this century, it is clear that one cannot negotiate in public without the serious risk that those negotiations will not succeed, and we want these negotiations to succeed in the interests of the people of Hong Kong as well as those of China and Britain. I believe that there is an understanding here and in Hong Kong that the talks must remain confidential. It may be frustrating for members and the people of Hong Kong not to know the precise details of what is happening in the negotiations and what is the British and Chinese posture, but it would be counter-productive if we were to start negotiating in public.

So with absolutely no indication of what was happening in the future, Hong Kong was voting with its airlines and tens of thousands of residents were becoming what was known colloquially as 'the yacht people', leaving the colony headed for Canada, the US, Britain and other countries, which ever offered the most convenient refuge. One South

American republic sold passports and residence to wealthy investors. The exodus went on and each year an estimated 30,000 people said farewell from the old Kai Tak Airport, clutching new documents allowing them to land in faraway homes. The British government was being pressured to provide a haven under a British Hong Kong passport classification following the Sino-British Joint Declaration that China would be taking sovereignty from the British in 1997.

There was also a burgeoning 'reverse' refugee situation at a time when boatloads of refugees from the communist rulers of Vietnam were making a dangerous crossing of the South China Sea with the bright lights of Hong Kong their beacon of hope. But for the incoming refugees, a long period of detention in prison camps awaited as the United Nations sought to find third country homes for them.

With friends I had a share in a motorised Chinese junk which we loaded with appropriate refreshment and congenial company most weekends and headed for some offshore island destinations, swimming and long lunches at seafood restaurants on Cheung Chau or Lamma Island.

In fact, living as a bachelor in Hong Kong could be likened to a kid in a lolly factory but occasionally one formed a longer relationship with the opposite sex and I still have fond memories of a Chinese lady of my acquaintance who not only played poker, but had lived in France and had some decidedly western traits that paved the way for a closer friendship. Obviously after many years I had a fair smattering of Cantonese, the rather guttural and tonal dialect that can sound screechingly offensive when shouted between two old ladies at opposite ends of a crowded mini-bus which was a popular 'hop-on, hop-off,' mode of commuting. But it was useful in just getting through an average day, buying in a street market, ordering a meal, or banter with a local colleague or directing a cab driver. The red diesel cabs were an essential and cheap means of city transport day and night. My lady friend had an accent much enhanced by her French domicile and we conversed in an exotic mixture of three languages. She was living on Cheung Chau Island that was remarkable for the fact it had no vehicles, just a series of narrow pedestrian lanes crisscrossing the homes of some 30,000 residents. Expats were attracted to cheaper rents just a ferry-ride from the CBD in the ambience of a fishing village.

Worth a mention is the Cheung Chau Bun Festival. If it had not been for my liaison of the time, it's probably not high on my bucket list but one of the few Chinese festivals with a fairground appeal. It centres around three towering bamboo structures laden in cakes and buns that after all sorts of parades and performances get clambered upon and the goodies distributed to those gathered. In my case, Western humour probably ended what had been a pleasant relationship. She was not amused when, with expat friends, I supervised a New Zealand export lamb we had acquired frozen at a city market roasting deliciously on a spit in the garden of a rented villa. Local Chinese were stopping and studying my strange occupation over the garden fence on their way here and there. I noted the interest and pointing at the sizzling and turning lamb I said in serious tones 'Lo Por, Hah. Lo Por'. That suggested it was my wife on the spit. No sense of humour of course. It wasn't long before the island police force arrived on their bicycles and I was thoroughly questioned and the meat carefully prodded and examined. I was rescued by my lady friend, but she decided I was just 'bloody chee sin gweilo' – or literally 'crossed wires white ghost idiot'. It's a pity. But in retrospect east and west have not really met in any permanent sense in my personal experience.

Speaking of humour I should mention here a pleasant Lamma Island shoreside luncheon at an establishment we dubbed the 'Lamma Hilton' for its popularity with us expats. It was a family-owned seafood restaurant and busy and bustling on most Sundays in particular. Hong Kong had an employment regime of five-and-a-half days, so Saturdays were too short for a proper day out on the water. I recall Tony spotting US TV star Larry Hagman at a crowded table on Lamma. The *Dallas* persona of J.R. Ewing was holding court and Tony could not help himself. On the wine list was a Chinese offering from the mainland, a white wine called Dynasty. The name on the label of course mirrored the opposition TV show currently listed against *Dallas* in the US and soon a Chinese waiter was delivering two such bottles to Ewing's table. I'll give the man credit when the waiter pointed us out. He smiled and nodded – just for a moment, before abruptly turning away.

Another more serious and waterborne incident was on Hong Kong's western approaches, and while these waters were patrolled by the Maritime Police in their high speed launches, there was busy traffic and some refugee craft got through the screen.

On one of our Sunday jaunts we cruised along off the island shores when we encountered an overcrowded boatload of Vietnamese who were in an old high-prowed vessel showing wear and tear as they waved frantically from off Lamma Island. They had escaped police attention and slipped into closer water. We were possibly open to a charge of aiding and abetting but we pulled alongside and threw what remained of our rather plentiful snacks and drinks across. Several children seized packets of chips, biscuits and bread rolls, tearing them open and cramming their mouths while adults downed bottled water, cans of beer and soft drink with cries of relief and broad smiles of thanks. Our boat boy Ah Chow, suddenly yelled 'bomban' (police inspector) and we saw a Marine Police launch heading our way. We veered off and watched as the refugee vessel was taken under tow and escorted away, pleased at least they'd had a semblance of welcome from us.

They had probably covered 1,000 kilometres on the barely-seaworthy vessel, fleeing poverty, and political repression. Nearly 200,000 Vietnamese would seek asylum in the city over the following years. Thousands more died trying to make the journey. My old friend from cadet days in New Zealand, the late John McBeth, was then based in Thailand as a freelance journalist and broke the story of the tragic and often grisly fate that too often ended attempts at freedom. He wrote with passion on the plight of refugees and war victims and in particular about the Thai pirates who raped and murdered Vietnamese boat people.

The United States started imposing stricter entry requirements on refugees in 1982 in a bid to slow the numbers accepted and found that many were simply economic escapees and even part of an orchestrated 'orderly departure scheme' with a blind eye policy supported by the Vietnamese government. The Hong Kong government finally had a policy of separating political from economic refugees and the latter were considered illegal immigrants and repatriated to Vietnam. I often wonder as to the fate of the boatload we encountered on our privileged Sunday outing on the sea because a few weeks after that encounter I visited a government closed camp at Sham Shui Po in the New Territories. It was apparent that the limited space of Hong Kong meant illegals were a serious problem. Behind prison-class high wire fences and razor-wire, they were housed in wooden barracks festooned with washing. Hundreds of men, women and children were crowded together in a heavily guarded facility made bleak to discourage messages of hope to a further influx of migrants.

A United Nations report described camp conditions as 'hell on Earth' and partially run by gangs. A companion walking the outside fence with me that day suggested the inmates might think home was a better place after all. Some asylum seekers stayed in the closed camps for years as they waited for a decision on their refugee status.

CHAPTER SIXTEEN

WHEN ARGENTINA INVADED the Falkland Islands in 1982 there was a burst of expatriate-led patriotic spirit. The British under Thatcher assembled a naval task force to recover what was after all, British soil, albeit many thousands of miles away in the South Atlantic. As the only comparable outlying colony, a kindred spirit was apparent in Hong Kong.

Working as assistant managing editor on TVB, and mindful of our English-speaking and 'ruling class government' audience, the Falklands fighting was pretty much the main news focus over the three months before the Argentines were battered into surrender in June, after bloody air, sea and land conflict. While there were many casualties of war, it became apparent that the local Chinese people had a substantial stake in the drama. It was estimated there were 400 Hong Kong crew among the 127 vessels that formed the convoys going south, employed in laundry, as tailors, seamen, trade technicians, fitters and cooks. In fact eight of them were killed in vessels hit by fire. One local man who did survive was presented with Britain's George Cross for bravery for carrying to safety servicemen injured in a fire on the ill-fated Sir Galahad when attacked by Argentine aircraft.

Wartime censorship was obviously the very stuff of HMG and our coverage on TVB relied on the BBC. Despatches from reporter, the late Brian Hanrahan had graphic details from the frontline but UK government lackeys and armchair warriors complained about the telling of troop and ship movements that informed the enemy. Hanrahan, who was later posted to BBC Hong Kong and was a fine fellow over a couple of beers, was lauded for his legendary phrase to avoid giving details on planes in a mission. He reported: "I counted them all out and I counted them all back in" describing a successful raid without allegedly breaking censorship numbers rules.

I spent a few days of sunny time-out in a neighbouring beach hut to Brian's in popular Puerto Galera in the Philippines and was impressed by the fact that even on the beach in a group of us enjoying cheap and good Tanduhay rum, slightly more expensive cold beers and barbecued king prawns, he remained glued to a small shortwave radio to keep in touch with world news. The job always came first.

International intrigue was often the stuff of life in Hong Kong and from my early days at United Press International in London and again in the first days with HMG I was very aware that the bloke in the bar of the Foreign Correspondents Club could be something more than the wire service hack he claimed to be. With its window on a still closed China – incidentally the distant best view in the world from the old Sutherland House harbour-facing men's urinal – Hong Kong was a veritable mecca and listening post for intelligence spooks from east and west.

Word soon came over the wires of some Europeans in trouble on the Spratley Islands off the Philippines. A Chinese 'outpost' had detained them, diplomatic phone wires had hummed and the men in question were being shipped to Hong Kong. They were met by an international media scrum and with a TV crew I was on a loaded ferry chartered by the Government Information Service, GIS, heading out to meet the rusty freighter carrying the strange passengers. But we were gazumped in good old fashioned news style by one Hugh Van Es. A rather profane and colourful Dutch-born photographer who was world famous for his dramatic rooftop helicopter ladder shot of panicked civilians as the Viet Cong captured Saigon, the late 'Vanes' joined a mate's live-aboard vessel and reached the gangway and close-up photos while we floated helplessly blocked from getting alongside.

At best we managed a distant TV camera shot of figures boarding Vane's boat. However there was a later press conference held at the Hilton Hotel. As our TVB crew gathered we drew curious looks from the many tourists, mainly Americans, relaxing in the main lobby lounge. I realised that my sound guy, Chinese reporter and two cameramen and I were as usual dressed in matching beige company issue safari suits, festooned with equipment. I was draped in spare battery belts, so we looked rather armed and intimidating in matching 'uniforms.' After the event it was obvious the self-described 'rescued fishermen' were intelligence operatives but in the way of such stories it soon faded away. But I include now a synopsis from the political front which shows even back then China was set on controlling the South China Sea. Now as I write in 2024, it's regarded as a flashpoint for armed conflict. Tony Baynes was an avid yachtsman back in those days and recalls:

I remember well on a trip back from the Philippines after the San Fernando or China Sea Race distinctly hearing the sound of what can only have been a submarine. It was a bright clear day and the noise could not have come from anywhere but underneath. Whose submarine it was we never knew, but all on board suspected China because the noise was so loud!

In May 1984, the Sixth National People's Congress in Bejing decided to establish the Hainan Administrative District. That in effect is today's contested area where China's unilateral South China Sea military installations include Nansha – the Spratlys where our European 'fishers' were detained by the People's Liberation Army and now a reclaimed fortified air base patrolled by PLA warships.

The Asian region continued its fascinating news cycle and I was building the 6pm news package at TVB when Benigno 'Ninoy' Aquino, the opposition leader during a decade of martial law under the Philippines President Ferdinand Marcos was assassinated in Manila in 1983. This political upheaval just 90 minutes flying time away saw news attention quickly focussed.

Planning to run for president,, Aquino was stymied by martial law and wound up in prison for eight years before, in the convoluted drama of Philippines politics, Marcos freed him to go into exile in the United States. Two years after martial law was lifted, Aquino flew home, intending to campaign in promised elections.

I kept a record after two days in Manila reporting the aftermath. In recent months there had been a shift in dynamics in his homeland. Marcos was in ill health and rumours spread of a private medical clinic being installed near his bedroom in the presidential palace. His perceived weakening led to opposition becoming bolder.

Aquino was fearful of civil war in his homeland, and was soon called upon to come back to link together the opposition forces ranging across the Philippines political spectrum. His supporters secured assurances from Marcos of his safe passage, but ignored warnings from the first lady, Imelda, that 'Aquino's enemies were everywhere'.

When he ignored the threat and flew home, military officers boarded the Japan Airlines Boeing 747 on the apron outside Manila terminal building and Aquino was quickly ushered off the aircraft. Journalists travelling with him were ordered to remain seated 'to enhance security'. As Aquino left the boarding steps to be met on the tarmac by an escort of soldiers from the Aviation Security Command, he was shot in the back of the head from a 357 Magnum revolver. He dropped, his head shattered, in his first step back onto Philippine soil. The killer dressed in the uniform of an airport baggage handler had in turn fallen under a convenient hail of automatic gunfire from the military escort. Aquino's body was rushed into the terminal building for futile medical attention.

A press release from Malacanang Palace later identified the gunman as a petty criminal who somehow evaded 'foolproof' airport security. Later in a Manila funeral home, a bulletproof vest was stripped from Aquino's body, proof that violence had not been unexpected.

Later, millions turned out across the nation to mourn Aquino and street demonstrations against the killing erupted. Martial law was declared. An independent commission concluded in October 1984 that a conspiracy led by the Philippine armed forces chief of staff, General Fabian Ver, was responsible but he and 25 co-conspirators were acquitted of these charges by three Marcos-appointed judges.

But the killing was the catalyst for Marcos's downfall and exile. In short a People's Revolution saw his palace fortress stormed by tens of thousands of citizens and the United State's flew in choppers from Clark Field to rescue him, his family and underlings. He was then flown to exile in Hawaii. In turn, Aquino's wife Corazon stepped up to the presidency.

Back in Hong Kong the business world produced a story worthy of a novel and a movie in the Carrian saga. It stuck in my mind for a conversation I had with an expatriate police superintendent after dinner at the Foreign Correspondents Club, now moved to grandiose premises in a converted warehouse in Hong Kong's Central District.

The Carrian Group came out of nowhere with

what seemed inexhaustible funding and invested in property locally and in many other counties. Some said it was Marcos money from the Philippines, but the truth was simpler when it crashed in a saga of murder and alleged suicide.

Through a series of companies Carrian had somehow secured massive bank loans with Malaysia's Bank Bumiputra in the gun for some $600 million. Things turned nasty when a Hong-Kong-based Bumiputra executive was found murdered by strangulation in a New Territories banana grove. Then in April 1984, a legal adviser to Carrian, an expat lawyer, was found dead in the swimming pool of his Hong Kong home. He had a manhole cover tied with a length of rope to his neck and his death was ruled a suicide. But my police informant, lubricated just a little, choked on his beer as he told me that two of his burly coppers could only just lift the concrete manhole cover between them. "You can't tell me that he tied himself to the cover and threw it in the pool," he said. "But what do I know, I'm just a plod, eh?" In those days in the colony, with HMG still at the helm, questioning a coroner's ruling could attract attention around visa renewal time. Reporters all remembered a classic 'death by suicide' ruling when a young expat police inspector, when homosexuality was still illegal on the local law books, killed himself in his government flat. It was ruled that he shot himself five times in his chest with his service revolver.

More news was made in another step on the road to a semblance of democracy aimed at a self-governing handover to China with HMG to be done and dusted just 12 years away.

In September 1985 the first ever election of the Legislative Council in Hong Kong 12 members were elected by Electoral Colleges and 12 by constituencies, while four official members and the rest of the seats were appointed by the Governor, Sir Edward Youde. I covered a number of LegCo sessions for TV, usually with a live cross from the steps of the council chamber via a remote link to the station. A quick visit to the bathroom to spruce up and check the jacket and tie would get the cameraman's blessing to proceed.

Sir Edward though would not survive to witness the result of his step towards local franchise as he became the only incumbent to die in office when he suffered a fatal heart attack in his sleep at the British Embassy in Beijing in the early hours of December 1986. Just a few weeks before in October he had seen Queen Elizabeth II as the the first British monarch to visit China in a gesture seeming to cement the takeover negotiations with some regal diplomatic gloss.

As ever, the weather kept us busy in Hong Kong and after my sojourn in television I was enticed away to work for the *Hong Kong Standard*, the English paper in opposition to the *South China Morning Post*, and owned by a Chinese entrepreneur, Sally Aw, heir to the substantial Tiger Balm fortune.

My move was in answer to a call from another lifelong friend, but sadly, now the late, Henry Parwani, something of a bilingual legend born of an Indian father and Chinese mum in the way of the melting pot of Asia. I remember as News Editor under Henry's watchful eye recording the progress of typhoon Wayne, one of the longest storms ever seen in Hong Kong and the general region of the north-west Pacific. For some three weeks from late August 1986 Wayne wandered back and forth just offshore with the Royal Observatory running typhoon signals up and down its mast. We escaped a direct hit, although across the region some 500 people lost their lives in heavy rains and high winds that ran up a damage bill of $400 million. I remember the drawn out tedium of weather from my front page headline 'Wayne, Wayne, Go Away!' I failed though to find a subtle Cantonese translation for 'Wayne, meaning rain' for some of my students from the Hong Kong Baptist College. They were regular journalism interns adding the role of mentor and English language news coach to my editing job.

This changed with the advent of a new Sally Aw title, *Extra*, a 16-page tabloid entertainment lift-out from the main daily paper and it fell to me to put the project together as Editor, a step up the corporate ladder. I formed a section of staff, promoted from within the existing complement and with four reporters and two designated subs established the new unit in an alcove of the extensive main newsroom. In my case it was a big learning curve being switched into the production process on a newly installed company-wide computer system. My days of typewriters, teleprinters and messengers were over, and I even had a fax machine!

Extra was a step into a new world for me after a career thus far focussed firmly on hard news. The product had an entertainment lifestyle as it's overriding brief in a city rather starved of anything but canto-pop with Chinese entertainers topping the local charts. As an English language publication, the international wires on the new computer set-up were rich pickings. British pop duo *Wham*, songwriter George Michael and instrumentalist Andrew Ridgley, had spent time in Hong Kong heading for a tour of China probably mixed up with HMG's diplomatic offensive over China's planned takeover.

When the two stars decided to go their separate entertainment ways, my front page of their large photo torn down the middle with the headline 'Wham Split' sold out that edition.

My reluctant introduction into the pop world saw me involved in a show by the legendary Commodores, sponsored to an outdoor concert at the Shatin Racecourse by newspaper magnate Sally Aw, ultimately of course my boss, But as an entertainment editor I was also a roving gofer for my work boss, my friend Henry Parwani whose family concert promotion company was behind the open air show. I recall having to hustle away in the office car, with driver, to locate some fresh new towels, after a Commodore member refused to go on stage in the Hong Kong heat and humidity without a supply. Not really the job for a senior journalist, I felt but figured Henry also had to be a 'gofer' under the circumstances.

Another showbiz note came as a friend and I were enjoying an Sunday ale on the Cheung Chau waterfront at a time when actor Sean Penn and new wife Madonna, were in Hong Kong and nearby Macau filming the movie *Shanghai Surprise*. They were playing a media blackout game and I had offered a HK$500 reward in *Extra* for information on their whereabouts. But as we sat in the sunshine, a couple of heavy-set European men walked past followed by Madonna and Penn, flanked by more bodyguards. Of course, my mate the late Vince Loden was a photographer. But it was 'his day off' and sans lens. In a panic he dived into a nearby shop trying to buy a disposable camera but failed to do so and we simply watched in professional frustration as the newlyweds stepped aboard a sampan ferry and it had to happen. Madonna slipped, tumbled into the sampan and fully exposed her knickers in doing so. No camera! The shot would have earned thousands of US dollars in the home media market.

As luck would have it we got a reply to my advert from the schoolboy son of a major hotel manager who was very happy with $500 pocket money and two of the newspaper's staffers on a hired motorbike managed to photograph Madonna on set in Macau. But of course the copyright was with the paper which sold the negatives in New York for a significant sum.

Another entertainment tabloid stunt I engineered almost made international headlines. It was April 1st, All Fool's Day, by tomorrow's edition and I was looking through the newspaper library for inspiration and came across an unusual photo. It was a uniformed British army sapper with a mine detector and headphones apparently sweeping a dolphin that had been hauled from an aquarium pool in a canvas bath. The incident was real and involved amusement park vets calling in the army and trying to locate a metal beer can that someone had thrown into the main pool and it was believed ingested by the dolphin.

However I quickly penned an elaborate story about how marine scientists based at Ocean Park, Hong Kong's aquaworld and amusement complex, had discovered the meaning of the dolpin's clicks and sonic squeaks and were able to translate these into human understanding. A 'high pitched sonic chattering' sound was actually a greeting between the species while various clicks indicated hunger, others amorous intent, sorrow, anger and so on. The photo added a realistic dimension and I made it a front page addition.

The international feedback came when Parwani rushed down to my section next morning with a Reuters newswire printout which carried a flash "cancellation to story xxx regarding Hong Kong dolphin breakthrough. Please note the date of this item. The error is regretted." or words to that effect. A bored night staffer in the Reuters Asian bureau had simply lifted the item for the wider world to read. Naturally we were all very pleased with ourselves and the item made good telling over a beer later at the FCC bar.

CHAPTER SEVENTEEN

BUT NOW FATE was to play a trick that changed my daily life for several long and rather dark months.

On a visit to the FCC, the normal foyer carpet was missing as I walked in towards the notorious main bar and a date with Hugh Van Es, 'Vanes' and his delightful wife Annie. She had christened me 'Pablo' and the name had stuck in our group of friends. However the parquet floor had been washed and polished with the carpet still to be replaced. My damaged right leg slipped suddenly from under me. I managed to grab the close-by bannister rail of a stairway leading up to the second floor restaurant with my right hand. As my legs slipped away I went sort of horizontal above the floor before gravity took over and there was a nasty 'pop'. The weight of my airborne body swung on my right arm and shoulder and the socket gave up the ghost. Simply, the doctor at a Happy Valley hospital informed me after the pain really set in, the fall had split in two the humeral head and damaged the articular cartilage.

He also had words to say about the bottled anaesthetic administered by my friends prior to realisation setting in, that real damage had been done.

After a spell in hospital, I was strapped up and semi-mobile. My gammy leg had taken a knock, but worse was the fact that my right arm played a specialised role in my overall gait, a balancing aid moving to compensate for my limp. In effect, I was a bit cast, particularly when it came to negotiating steps or stairs, an integral part of the urban landscape.

In short, I had to take some leave. As it progressed I found myself often at a high stakes poker evening in the basement games room of the FCC. In fact, the game of seven card stud, High-Low seemed to suit me. I was soon making my salary equivalent and more. That progressed to another high stakes game above a Central restaurant that attracted a contingent of jockeys from the Happy Valley racing stables. I still held my own but envied the jockeys when one of their number fell short in the game. His mates muttered consolingly that he could bet on his own mount by proxy in the last race next Saturday. They would pull their mounts and he would be allowed to win.

The local racing industry was a case of who you knew, not what you knew. While on *Extra* I had an invitation to join a major Chinese trading company as they hosted Captain Mark Phillips, Princess Anne's first husband. He was dubbed 'Fog' as some unkind person described him as 'thick and wet'. Anyway, I watched without much surprise as he was escorted by his hosts to the corporate box betting window and helped to place his bets. The three horses his hosts selected for him won in fine style.

When another guest asked to jump on the bandwagon, they shook their heads. It seemed the quota of wins was completed. Still, I did enjoy the mulligatawny soup and roast beef luncheon and the Rolls Royce courtesy car homewards.

As my shoulder healed I confessed to slipping down a slippery slope and decided to resign from my job, a decision reinforced by the arduous travel and stairs involved in my daily commute of an hour to the Standard building in a factory complex in the outskirts of Kowloon.

Thus my life revolved around card games interspersed with some freelance writing for colleagues seeking help on magazines and trade publications.

One freelancing assignment was to provide a potted tour of the Wanchai bar district, a back-handed compliment to my supposed in-depth knowledge from late night excursions therein. While this excerpt I wrote for the tourist-oriented book *Another Hong Kong Explorer's Guide* harks back to the 1980's it does provide a glimpse of night-life life we experienced in the old days.

I wrote:

> Hong Kong's night-life cannot be completely experienced without a visit to Wanchai with its two glittering blocks of disco bars, girly bars, short time hotels and the odd 'massage parlour' thrown in. It's perhaps a tawdry remnant of the once famous strip which had its heyday during the Indochina War, but it's still a must visit. Demographics have changed since Susie Wong of the movie era but Susie's topless sisters or daughters are still there in diehard speakeasies hidden behind faded velvet curtains.
>
> They'll calculate your monthly salary by the cut of your suit and proceed to fleece you accordingly. But the top of the line is the disco pub and here the demographic influence

comes into play. Hong Kong in the last decade has become home to an increasing number of Filipina domestic workers. There is one thing they love more than anything and that's music and the mix makes nocturnal magic if you are loose and out after dark.

Perhaps the best place to begin our wander through the Wanch is The Wanch itself, a folk club that begins to liven up with the after-work crowd of expatriate locals probably because of an extensive 'happy hour' until 8pm. Someone will pick up a guitar around 9pm to keep you entertained while the action warms up elsewhere.

If you feel inclined to move on, the first port of call will probably be the Suzie Wong club just around the corner in Fenwick Street. Now you are heading into more dangerous territory. There's a basic rule of thumb for those who work in Hong Kong's girlie bars and that is to get as much money out of the punter in as short a time as possible. With that fact of life firmly implanted in your mind, proceed. A beer, usually a can which is true of all the red light bars, will cost a little more than the standard price. You'll be pestered for a drink by a Chinese, Filipina, or Thai hostess and this is where caution should prevail. If you are tired and emotional enough to weaken, stipulate the price. They can be three or four times the price of your beer and escalate therefrom frighteningly and are merely cold tea. There are three girly bars in the short Fenwick

Street block – Suzy Wong Club, the An An Club, and The Club Gold Star.

If you can tear yourself away, slip upstairs next to the An An to the Pussycat Disco-pub. Here raven haired young ladies from the Philippines hold sway, especially on Sundays when some 40,000 have the same day off across the colony. A live band starts playing at 9pm belting out rock'n'roll and disco hits over a central dance floor and two bars dispense the necessary. Drinks are generally priced a little higher than standard. The place is well run by an elderly mamasan at the door, name of Sweetwater. Any red blooded male will soon find a dance partner and long lasting relationships have been established here. For a mixed group, the Pussycat also provides an acceptable atmosphere.

There is a more European flavour at our next stop, the venerable Crossroads pub-disco in the basement on the corner of Fenwick Street at Lockhart Road. Servicemen from local defence forces and visiting warships seem to have made this place their own and late at night it is not for the faint hearted. There's a cover charge, a free drink, disco music and a lot of noise. Prices are similar to those of the Pussycat.

A few steps down Lockhart Road brings us to Neptune which for some reason has the reputation for attracting the best looking crowd early in the evening. And prices are aligned with venues already mentioned. In the wee hours it's raunchy and when those from the twilight zone hold court. There's a strong Filipina contingent once again with a sprinkling of semi-professional Thai ladies and off duty nightclub hostesses. The bar is supported by wan-faced expatriates be they world weary or just off a night shift at one of the two English language morning newspapers. A live band keeps things rocking along.

Across Lockhart Road is the One For Two smallish disco club often with the best band to be found on the Strip. The clientele here has been known to include a covert lesbian segment. We're now into the tail end of the night and it's perhaps worth a trip or stumble back down Lockhart Road to the east of Luard Road. Here the last remnants of the Vietnam era are still hanging on in three clubs – Country Laser, Popeye Topless and San Francisco. Leotard clad lovelies from Thailand and the Philippines gyrate on platforms behind the bar while somewhat frumpy hostesses vie for your remaining dollars.

From here on in, it's mostly down-hill, with the remaining bars on the opposite side of the road on a subsistence living waiting for a floating high roller to empty his wallet or bruise his credit card. They may be worth a look but keep in mind that it's your cash they are after, not your heart. Those might be goldfish in the tank behind the bar but the piranhas are hustling drinks.

A late night-early morning meal is often

a good idea to soften the hangover looming ahead. Last stop leads us down Lockhart to the internationally renowned Horse and Groom, known locally as 'The House of Doom'. Here the flotsam and jetsam of the night have found a peaceful harbour after a stormy passage of the evening. With your last cold beer, tuck into a plate of the best steak, eggs and chips in town – well surely, it is at 5am. When they throw you out the door it is probably daylight.

Of course that was a pretty sanitised version because sometimes Wanchai was not for the delicate. I recall one early morning enjoying a reviving steak at the House of Doom at a time when the US 7th Fleet was in port for R and R. Well some bright spark had allowed the Scots Guards resident garrison squaddies loose from Port Stanley barracks at the same time. I had noticed clashes between servicemen earlier and the local cops had actually barricaded part of Lockhart Road where a bit of an international military melee had broken out. But then the pub door opened and in staggered about 50 feisty battered and somewhat bloody Scots Guards demanding beer and a sit down. One had what seemed to be a broken-off wooden bar stool leg as a club. Outside, a bunch of yanks were in full cry, but then a British Army bus pulled up at the door and a giant of a regimental colour sergeant in full uniform and red sash with visored hat pulled low over his eyes stepped down. He stood in the doorway and roared: "Are yee tha Scots Guaaards thun?" The squaddies leapt to attention. "On tha BUUUSS" roared the sergeant. They did so and out the door I saw the US sailors moving away as local cops formed a line from the door. The squaddies marched out as the sergeant sought two cases of beer from the barman. "Bill tar Fooort" he commanded and re-boarded the bus to applause from his troops. We carried on with our meal.

On another occasion a mate and I had to step over a Chinese male lying in a pool of blood outside a particular bar only frequented by Hong Kong local lads. There were other men, probably triad gangsters, emerging from the bar door. He could have been alive or dead but to stop and investigate was inviting confrontation.

There was one safe haven when out very late at night for those in the know and that was the Professional Club. This was a speakeasy behind a locked door upstairs in a Kowloon commercial building run by an Asia legend, Neva Shaw, an American diva who had many years across Asia after an entertainment stint in wartime Vietnam. The Pro-Club was a gathering place for those souls employed in the bars and clubs or other night haunts including 'professional' ladies of the night and journalists off night shift. It was a rather fascinating venue and perhaps it's sufficient to say that what 'goes on tour, stays on tour'.

CHAPTER EIGHTEEN

OF COURSE LATE nights in Wanchai and elsewhere had nothing to do with things but I also soon discovered that professional gambling which I considered a viable option to work, proved otherwise. My stake dwindled. But serendipity was with me in an approach from a publishing house. I included many walks of life among my friends and contacts and was offered the job of taking over from a Canada-bound executive editor and I accepted, sensible at last, to find myself with a stable of four prestigious magazine titles. I blessed my *South Africa Review* experience of Canberra days and set to productive work once more with Thompson Press Hong Kong Ltd. My magazines, supported by a secretary and excellent local staff, were *Premier*, for gold card customers of the monolithic Hong Kong and Shanghai Bank, *Visa Magazine* for lesser cardholders, as well as region-wide *Asian Hotel and Catering Times* and *Asian Architect and Contractor*. *Premier* was bi-monthly while the remainder were monthly issues, so it was busy.

Funnily enough, just weeks into the new role, Henry Parwani reached out for me to staff a new Sally Aw project, a monthly magazine *China Review* as a window on the huge next door neighbour that was to become Big Daddy. But he understood I had made an honest commitment, despite trying to entice me with more money.

I soon settled in to Thompson Press and it wasn't

long before the fringe benefits of running the four publications started polishing my lifestyle. *Premier Magazine* with its high-end target readership carried top advertising and copy to match. With the latter came expensive luncheons and dinners as public relations and advertising agencies lobbied for editorial exposure. *Visa* had its own PR catchment and such offerings as catered box seats at the Hong Kong Rugby Sevens, the forerunner of today's international series.

Hotel and Catering Times was designed as an Asia-wide circulation, with similar PR hustles for space, such as free airfares and accommodation at five star hotels from Singapore, to Bangkok to Tokyo – and even New York for an industry convention.

It was not possible to accept the majority of such offers, but Hong Kong hotel hospitality was a different matter. I would soon lose track of 'freebies'. In fact, on one occasion at the end of the office day at 5pm, I contemplated 15 invitations to cocktail parties, buffet and top hotel restaurant meals from the ubiquitous city hotel PR platoon, and instead scurried home to my small high rise flat and a can of beer and a toasted cheese sandwich.

But there was one dinner event I attended that will remain with me forever.

I was invited to attend a farewell for the outgoing general manager and also the food and beverage manager of the iconic Peninsula Hotel, arguably the premier establishment in the city, to be held at the acclaimed Gaddis Restaurant.

I arrived in suitable formal attire to find myself

seated with a lady from the British press, M. Jaques and Mme Pebeyre, who were major exporters of truffles from France, and the two hotel executives. What followed at our table in the centre of Gaddis with the maître d' in charge of six personal waiters standing behind each chair, was mind-blowing. There were seven courses, all but the sorbet and dessert featuring lashings of truffles, from the appetiser of toasted truffle cocktail sandwiches, through to some form of truffle tart and on to Angus steaks a la lashings of truffles.

But it was the wine list that topped things gastronomic. The loyal staff of 'The Pen', as the Japanese invaded the colony in December 1941, spirited away the extensive cellars that had been laid down in the 20's and buried the carefully wrapped wines in a New Territories paddy field. With liberation in 1945, the bottles were carefully exhumed and returned intact to the hotel basement. It was a selection of these wines that appeared from the cellars again and I had to note an early Chateau Mouton Rothschild, presumably true to label in such a prestigious location. It was one of a dozen vintages during the course of the dinner and today, if it could be found, could cost up to several thousand US dollars.

At around midnight, with a coffee and liqueur nightcap with the F&B manager, I ventured the question: "What would be my bill if I repeated this meal next week?" He simply smiled. "If you possibly could, and actually you could not duplicate it exactly, you'd be looking at..." he thought for a minute and had a whispered consultation with his outgoing GM, both bound for top roles at the Bangkok Oriental in Thailand, then said "Say US$1,200 per head, six people, some wines extra. You'd be looking at about US12,000."

Well, 'The Pen' got a jolly good write up in the next issue of *Premier*.

On another occasion, my then 12-year-old son Shaun was visiting me from his boarding school in Sydney, Australia and it coincided with a complimentary suite at the Mandarin Hotel in Central District. The PR lady concerned was happy to include him so I was pretty chuffed to host my son in a penthouse level suite complete with butler service. The freebie was aimed at publicising the hotel's upcoming VIP package and included a Rolls Royce shopping trip and a helicopter ride over the city from the HMS Tamar Naval Base near the hotel. The flight was complete with Sony Walkman's and appropriate music, in my case Tchaikovsky, and Shaun, even though a last minute inclusion in the exercise, had a Rick Astley tape to suit his pre-teen taste. He rose to the occasion though and calmly ordered abalone for his evening meal – at around US$100 a pop – at the 25th floor Pierre Restaurant.

Shaun's visit was doubly highlighted when he accompanied me on a visit to the USS Enterprise aircraft carrier when the American Seventh Fleet again visited town. The US public relations people reached out and accompanied by the carrier's executive officer I was invited as an editor to visit on board. In fact Shaun had the VIP treatment, sitting in the cockpit of an F14, and also shown into a restricted navigation area, with his father held back by a Marine sentry. "Ok for kids only," he said simply.

The magazine stable was a passport to the high life, it might seem, but in fact a major international news break soon saw me thrust back in the front line in an event that reverberated around the world and one that I was involved in by proximity to the main event.

June 3rd 1989 is the day the Chinese rulers destined to run Hong Kong dealt with a peaceful protest by mobilising troops and gunning down hundreds, if not thousands, of people who had taken to the streets in and around Beijing's Tiananmen Square in a vain call for political change.

Student demonstrations had been growing for a couple of months and were being watched closely in Hong Kong with mounting approval and sympathy from local Chinese and expatriates alike. But after talks between the demonstrators and the Chinese government to find a peaceful resolution failed, the authorities declared martial law on the night of June 3rd. As those shots were heard around the world along with dramatic television footage, including that of a lone male student facing down a column of PLA tanks, demonstrations protesting the Chinese apparent massacre erupted from all points of the compass.

Work in my office became virtually impossible as my staff seemed to take on a mass reaction, ranging from impotent but vociferous anger to anguished tears. I pretty much declared a holiday and decided to head for the Press Club to compare notes with my colleagues. The club situated conveniently in the heart of Wanchai had become a popular alternative to the more expensive and high profile FCC with its huge non-media corporate and associate membership. It was made more so on the arrival as Press Club manager of Pip, Tony Baynes' elder sister, for a Hong Kong stay. Her culinary skills leading to English roast dinner lunches were well patronised by both expat and local news people.

I soon heard reports from Chinese media colleagues that local action was to follow the shocking events in Beijing.

So while demonstrations erupted throughout the world in the days following the initial crackdown, people in Hong Kong formed a massive rally, one of the largest in local history, to mourn the dead and protest the Chinese government action. A movement which cobbled together various organisations and trade unions launched more than 1.5 million people in a march through the streets in the world's largest protest outside Beijing.

I stood on a street corner, hand on my heart, as the local people were joined by a sprinkling of expat businessmen and women and probably a few enthusiastic tourists. I didn't march, fearful of my damaged leg in the large movement of people.

Prior to the 1997 Chinese takeover in Hong Kong, the memorial march became an annual event. However if nothing else, the mainland led to a more general exodus from Hong Kong of some long-standing expats I had known for 15 years, all citing an uncertain future, especially where families were concerned.

CHAPTER NINETEEN

I WAS MULLING over the future when on July 16th 1990, a magnitude 7.8 earthquake struck the main island of Luzon in the Philippines, causing widespread devastation and loss of life in the Baguio region north of Manila.

I flew to Manila two days later on a cover story for *Asian Architect and Contractor Magazine*, as some of the mag's board of governors were headquartered there.

Common sense dictated a base for myself in the Nikko Hotel, specifically designed for the Japanese owner as an earthquake resistant structure. I appreciated the fact as a series of aftershocks sent tremors through the city, making my snatched sleep a little restless. I have quoted here my story filed a week later headed *'Devastation in the Philippines'*. It is a fuller account in the context of this memoir simply because I have always said today's news is tomorrow's wrapping paper and this was so true in this case. A week after the quake, the world's attention had dramatically and firmly switched to the Middle East as Saddam Hussein lined up 100,000 soldiers to invade Kuwait.

The Philippines disaster was pushed from world headlines. Hopefully my account filed from Manila went in some way to make some media amends.

> Dateline Manila: At the time of writing the death toll from the 7.8 Richter scale shock that hit the Philippines is 1,800 dead and still rising with

1,000 confirmed missing and 117,000 homeless. In fact, the full loss of life will probably never be accurately known because perhaps hundreds of bus passengers, transport drivers and occupants of private cars and jeepneys for hire are buried forever under mountains, which simply slipped across the three highways connecting the region with the outside world. Apart from the two major quake centres, there are towns and villages throughout the region where the cost is still to be counted. In some communities, town centres sank up to four metres, destroying infrastructure and electrical services.

Hard on the heels of the disaster came rainstorms and flooding adding to the chaos, misery and damage to property. Initially, the relief action from the rest of the country was hesitant with communications in complete disorder. It wasn't until appeals for help were broadcast on local radio stations and picked up in Manila 218 kilometres to the south that the enormity of the tragedy became apparent. Manila was busy counting the cost of its own quake experience, somewhat diluted from the intervening countryside. The shock still rattled across the capital, demolishing several old low storey buildings and killing 36 people. But largely the city was unscathed, although nine public schools have had to close because of structural damage. All construction work was also halted on buildings that had reached two storeys so that structural engineers could carry out checks.

Back in the quake zone proper those in the resort city of Baguio, were beginning to make contact with the outside world through cellular telephones, and the office of President Corazon Aquino began to coordinate rescue operations. Initial help came from the American armed forces stationed at nearby Clark air base and Subic Bay naval base. Teams were helicoptered in to begin probing rubble for survivors.

The Philippine Contractors Association swung into action with an emergency meeting and President Jose Angeles told me the association's immediate course of action was to offer men and machinery to the government rescue operation. "A 19 man team of professionals was put together including structural engineering experts to go to Baguio to help direct rescue operations," he said.

"The specialised knowledge in the construction of buildings possessed by the team was held in abeyance for an agonising four days as the priority was placed on men by the government." He said many lives that were lost could well have been saved if this team had received the necessary priority to be flown in, in the initial stages. "Many of the initial rescuers were simple soldiers both American and Filipino. Their efforts were obviously heroic but provision should have been made to get people in who could direct them on where to work on a damaged building with some safety and some chance of success. 'Work was underway to clear a series of highway landslides, some up to half a mile long, but a series of aftershocks rocked the region and new landslides came down to close that which had been cleared.'

In the new masthead *AAC Magazine* my subsequent editorial reflected on a sad saga.

There is an image seared into my soul of a child's arm sticking out from between two concrete floor slabs concertinaed in a Baguio school collapse, a photograph I deemed too graphic to use in my report. I left it to Philippine media colleagues to probe reports that President Aquno's staff delayed vital relief supplies, tents, blankets and clothing and food, to wrap parcels in yellow coverings – because yellow was the presidential campaign colour.

But a final thought is a photo I took of a Baguio street in ruins. My esteemed mate Tony Baynes thought it was a 'bloody good piccie'. He had recently left radio for a high flying corporate role and more with Coca Cola International and was in Manila when I was, but busy co-ordinating the local franchise relief efforts that included getting bottled water into the quake zone. My street photo showed the only thing still standing upright – a pole with a red and white Coke sign atop.

It was almost as though that quake assignment put an appropriate question mark on my own future. I certainly loved Hong Kong, possibly too much so for a free-wheeling lifestyle, as much as professional satisfaction. It was a vibrant city with its myriad pleasures of the flesh as well as the mind and one 'worked hard and played harder'. It was made easy too. I remember after a long lunch on a Friday deciding to start the weekend early. I rang my secretary with the conversation going something like this.

"Hi Rosemary. Mr Campbell here. Any calls?"

"Ah, Sir, Mr Cammell not here. Not can call."

"No no. Rosie No Mr Campbell here speaking and has he missed anything. Any problems there?"

"Ahh, no, Mr Cammell not missing, he go lunch and not here for speaking. No problem for him."

It just seemed easier to go back to the bar.

Meantime in the Middle East it seemed like World War Three was gearing up and after a total of too many years in Kong Kong I started missing friends who'd seen China's writing on the wall and made tracks for places like Los Angeles and London, Manila and Sydney or places in between. There was also the fact that at 44 years of age I was still hireable, but would that be the same when China took over and I would be 51? Hmmm. Cutting a long story short again I began a round of farewells, usually in a bar somewhere and over a few cold beers with an old and good friend of long standing, I talked myself into making a move. He was Kiwi journalist extraordinaire, the late Kevin Sinclair, convivial from days in Canberra when he worked for Australian Truth in Melbourne and on to Hong Kong and the South China Morning Post before freelancing including writing extensively for some of my magazines. He also had a successful sideline writing, of all things, cook books. Kevin scored an OBE in the HMG honours list, for 'services to journalism in Hong Kong' and was quoted at the time as saying he "left New Zealand for the simple reason there was maybe only one murder a year to report on." A designated gong aside, a favourite story he repeated over beers was when he sent a local reporting team to check an alleged oil spill from a passing tanker in Repulse Bay, a popular beach swimming spot. When the reporter and photographer found no sign of oil, he instructed them to call into the nearby Stanley village market, buy a couple of frozen whole fish and toss them in the water for a quick photo. 'Oil Spill Kills Fish' ran the headline. Services to journalism can vary depending upon necessity.

Kevin was diagnosed with throat cancer during the time I worked for HMG. While undergoing radiation therapy at Queen Mary Hospital near my Baguio apartment, he would call in and raid the fridge for a cold beer to soothe things after a session. When finally surgery was required and he had to carry a notebook to communicate until a semblance of voice control was developed by literally 'burping', he was interviewed by a visiting newsman in the FCC. Kevin was writing his answers down and the out-of-town chap for some reason then started writing his questions and handing them to Kevin. The next note he got back was, in capital letters: 'I CAN'T SPEAK BUT I AM NOT FUCKING DEAF.'

As mentioned, Kevin thought New Zealand was too quiet for a newshound like him and he wondered if I would have the same problem. I was soon to recall his concern.

CHAPTER TWENTY

ONE RAINY AND misty Hong Kong September day in 1990, I took a taxi to Kai Tak airport. For perhaps the last time for the foreseeable future, the Air New Zealand Boeing took me out to the west over the harbour and southwards. I was already back in New Zealand when in the mail I received a sort of epitaph in the *Hong Kong TV Times* gossip column, which simply read: 'Paul Campbell it appears, after putting up with Hong Kong for longer than anyone can remember has quietly slipped away 'to parts unknown".

Initially I was agreeing with Kevin's view of our home country. Several times in fact, I regretted my decision to return and it was only family contact that eased me into a rather lackluster environment. For a couple of months I opted to freelance for a crust while looking around for lucrative employment. A couple of approaches to similar local trade publications I'd edited, like *Cuisine Magazine*, prompted an observation that I was 'too experienced and would probably soon want to move on to something better.'

It was then that Kevin Sinclair's OBE observation was rather blown out of the water. On November 13th that year, 13 souls met their end in a hail of high velocity gunfire in a small seaside village at Aramoana, in the deep south near Dunedin in the deadliest mass murder in New Zealand history.

David Gray was a reclusive out-of-work 33-year-old local man who had a verbal altercation with a neighbour. That led to him returning from his shack with a rifle and killing the man and his daughter. After that, in sniper movie style, he shot anything that moved within his range through a telescopic sight As his victims fell, emergency calls were made and police were soon on the scene. The first officer there also died. The siege lasted until the next day when an armed offenders unit surrounded a house. Gray burst out firing his weapon and he fell mortally wounded by police fire.

It was pre-email time for me, but with news of this magnitude it was worth a phone call to Kevin in Hong Kong and I quickly had a call back from Henry Parwani who took details and immediately relayed these to his contacts. In short, I scooped the international media with a breaking news cover in several Chinese language media outlets. Next day international media syndicates flocked to report the event.

The mass killing inevitably provoked talk of gun control and a 1992 amendment to the regulations on military-style semi-automatic firearms. Fast forward however to March 2019 and 51 people massacred in the Christchurch mosque attacks. There was another knee-jerk gun amnesty. But a duck-hunting shotgun or a rabbit-shooting .22 calibre is deadly. It is the man, not the weapon, that kills.

My efforts at gainful employment took a sudden turn and enforced the adage that it's not what you know, but who. In 1992 I suddenly found myself back in radio, and some time thereafter, in television as well. I was contacted by a friend from Radio Hauraki days and before long the following article appeared in a Sunday newspaper headlined:

Echoes from the past go to air

Five radio Hauraki jocks from the pirate and immediate post pirate days have regrouped to hit the airwaves again on Auckland International Airport station 1476 am The five, Mike Jack, Jim Smith, Paul Campbell, Tom Clark and Barry Knight, share 150 years of broadcasting among them and are covering shifts from breakfast to drive time.

Ironically, they're broadcasting on their old Hauraki frequency and using Hauraki's two original transmitters. The veterans have worked around the world and New Zealand since they quit Hauraki at various times in the 70s. So when the last, Barry Knight, joined the Airport station a few days ago, the five decided the story was too uncanny not to tell. They claim Airport Radio had to pay them 'huge sums of money', to move them out of early retirement. But their operations manager Mike Jack says "that's wishful thinking on their part."

The report was accompanied by a photo of the five of us waving enthusiastically from around a station-logoed vehicle.

But sadly it was a short lived affair of six months or so, with advertising, a station's lifeblood, falling short of the expectations of airport management and the station closed with staff offered positions elsewhere on the wider locale. One lass became a flight terminal advice announcer. Before shutdown though, Tom and I ran what we reckoned was the best hour of news on the airwaves at 5pm, aimed at commuters heading home with the car radio on. We did a tandem read, interspersed with the odd observation and it was well received as were the other on air staff. We had fun too. When the airport decided to stage an air show, with all sorts of exotic craft including a Harrier Jump jet, I recalled an old Hauraki promotions guy, Mike Baker, saying that "on radio you can drop a giant cherry from a helicopter on top of Rangitoto island made of icecream and marshmallow. It's the stuff of imagination."

Accordingly Tom and I, after a few beers at the hospitality tent, commandeered an electric golf buggy with a windscreen. Tom did a live cross to Nerida Nicols in the studio, claiming to be in a helicopter overhead, while I paddled the windscreen to the beat of a chopper rotor blade.

Dear Nerida joined the fun by reporting our location, 'over the far end of the runway folks!'

However, the station manager, the lovely late Robyn Johnson, thought otherwise and in my case sent me home in a taxi, suggesting too much hospitality tent was to blame.

With the demise of Airport Radio, for the next couple of years I reported for work each weekend for a two-day stint as relieving Foreign Editor at TV3, the independent national channel having been tapped for the vacancy by my old Radio Hauraki colleague and good friend from sailing days Mike Brockie who was the Associate News Director. As New Zealand was first to see the daily sun rising, the news of the rest of the world had just made the major evening bulletins so I had BBC, ITN and American networks to edit from for local consumption. Occasionally there were satellites to arrange for updated news feeds and in one memorable case, a ringside seat at a Los Angeles news drama that concluded just in time to make our 6 pm news lead story.

In June 1994 former American Football star player OJ Simpson hit prominence for a different reason entirely with the murders of his ex-wife Nicole Brown, and her friend, Ronald Goldman. Their bodies were found on a pathway outside Nicole's apartment building. Police said they found DNA evidence that supported the presumption that Simpson had been involved in the killings and said they wanted Simpson to turn himself in. Instead O.J. Issued a statement saying in part:

> I have nothing to do with Nicole's murder. I loved her, always have and always will. If we had a problem, it's because I loved her so much. I've had a good life. I'm proud of how I lived. Don't feel sorry for me. I've had a great life, great. Please think of the real O.J. and not this lost person.

Public reaction when this was broadcast led many to believe OJ was planning to commit suicide What followed was a dramatic live-on-television slow motion car chase through Los Angeles. Simpson's Ford Bronco was seen on an interstate highway being driven by his friend Al Cowlings with OJ in the back seat holding a pistol to his head. Police talked by cell phone while the car procession was taking place pleading with him to stop and surrender. In Auckland and around the world, TV stations were monitoring the event as the cops followed the Bronco at snail-like speed, The Dukes of Hazzard this was not. People alerted by newscasts crowded onto LA overpasses to watch as the Bronco passed them followed by patrol cars and news helicopters. The chase finally ended at Simpson's home where he finally listened to his close friend, surrendered to the police and was arrested. This happened with something like five minutes to go before TV3's main news at 6pm and it was a flurry of editing and typing into the computer system to get the full report to air and lead the news with seconds to spare. The adrenalin comedown took an after-work beer or two.

It was around this time in 1994 or 1995 that a rather life and work changing development took place as the Internet and email began to increase in prominence over the formerly closed circuit production machines of my experience. I bought a personal computer and signed up for email, and suddenly found a new lease of life in personal communication with old and good friends from across the world and in writing.

A freelance journalism occupation suddenly became viable and possibly rewarding. But a long standing desire to write a book, while now made easier by technology, would have to wait until I padded the coffers to take some time out. Weekends at TV3's foreign desk barely paid the rent, so I took stock, and as happens in life, a great opportunity came my way.

CHAPTER TWENTY-ONE

AN EMAIL FROM old Hong Kong mates, journo's Bruce MacDonald and Ferdie Stolsenberg, invited me to join an adventure and go with them on a 'fishing trip' to the Tubbataha Reef, deep in the Sulu Sea, in the southern Philippines.

It was a time when the Chinese incursion into the South China Sea was attracting world media attention. By tagging along I figured there were a number of good stories for magazine clients at least, so counted the dollars involved and signed on with my erstwhile friend and colleague Adrian Blackurn, who wrote the book on Radio Hauraki mentioned previously. He was between his rather long list of wives and with grown children was always ready to travel.

Before we left, Sandy MacDonald who had lived and worked in the immediate region tried to put something of a damper on our enthusiasm.

"Let me tell you something," said Sandy when we imbibed at the popular Northcote Tavern, "when I was editing the *Borneo Bulletin*, these two bancas full of pirates armed with automatic weapons came ashore at one of the towns in Sabah. They just drove up on the beach, then headed into the centre of town, firing as they went. Within twenty minutes they had cleaned out two banks and were headed out to sea again. Thirty two dead. And there was hardly a word in the press anywhere else in the world. This sort of thing was just too common. Now just let me say it again. Don't do it."

But we did. I flew solo to Manila, and by some alchemy, Blackburn flew in from a European assignment quite independently and in a domestic terminal teeming with a thousand travelling Filipinos, as though we'd made an appointment, he tapped my shoulder from behind and plumped down on a bench beside me. I'd expected perhaps to link up at a Puerto Princessa hotel much later.

The Sulu Sea was an eye-opener. A local expat charter operator come beach-comber pointed us aboard a native banca, some 60 feet of narrow hull supported by outriggers. Bruce, Adrian and myself were soon 90 kilometres out at sea moored off a small island at the end of a long reef littered with rusting shipwrecks. But we were missing one of our party. Ferdie Stolsenberg had not made the cut. He was an Aussie, but German-born and a fluent speaker, who had missed the scheduled flight. But he chartered a private plane and then strangely enough arrived aboard a Philippines Coast Guard swept up modern banca, complete with an armed escort, to join our party. And he had two corpulent gentlemen in tow that can only be described as 'fat German spies'. It made for a crowded boat with a cabin that might sleep four at a pinch, with a crew of four locals who at least slept on deck forward of the cabin. There was room in the stern for extra bodies.

The Sulu sea basin stretches between the Visayas Archipelago, Sabah, and Borneo and is 400 kilometres wide, isolated for the most part with just two small islands north and south of the Tubbataha Reef. We had been briefed in Manila by a conservationist group who explained that unsustainable fishing practices had hurt commercially significant species and affected reef health. Corals and coral stones were mined despite laws prohibiting this and illegally smuggled to Europe for the aquarium industry. There was also a suggestion that when Marcos was in power, people tried to stop the smuggling of live exotic fish to Hong Kong. They say Marcos 'taxed' that lucrative illegal trade and when opposition reared its head, simply threatened to cancel Philippine Airlines routes to the region. This was the situation in the mid-1990s, but perhaps it's improved all these years later after being designated a national treasure. Unesco's World Heritage Centre calls the Tubbataha Reef Marine Park 'an excellent example of a pristine coral reef with lagoons and two coral islands'.

When Ferdie arrived we had been on our banca for two days, having little space for rest and a blocked very primitive toilet in the small cabin amidships. Toilet was a matter of hanging in the water under an outrigger beam when nature demanded. The two German chaps seemed disinterested in fishing and more concerned with binoculars and cameras. And asking questions. However after another day in the hot sun, Blackburn and I decided to hitch a ride on the coast guard patrol which was heading home to Palawan. Before I gathered my few belongings to leave for civilisation I recorded this vignette of our fishing success:

Secrets of the Sulu Sea

It came over the stern in a twisting snapping fury

of spray, 5cm fangs seeking bloody vengeance. A hundred miles offshore in the Philippines Sulu Sea, on a metre-wide banca stern, there is nowhere to hide. But somehow, we found cover as our boat boy Louie dealt to the writhing 20 kilo barracuda with 'the Filipino anaesthetic', a rusty spanner used as a brain-shattering billy club. We were trailing our lures off Tubbataha Reef, perhaps the loneliest fishing spot in the world. Deep into the 7,000 islands of the Philippines, is one of Asia's best kept secrets, probably because it is not for the squeamish.

On the way back with the coastguard, we got up close and personal with the Sulu's Sea Gypsies. These extended families led their lives in bancas moored up on the water with fish and coral gathering their 'apparent' only income. One of their young men dived in and swam to our craft trailing a bunch of fresh-caught fish that he threw over the gunnels as an offering to the uniformed guard. He was acknowledged with a wave by Corporal Urban Evangalista, our friendly armed escort. The gypsies of course would have been related to the sea raiders that our mate Sandy Macdonald warned us about. On the final leg to shore, Evangalista fired the contents of the magazine of his automatic rifle in a fusillade over the stern, a demonstration of course that he had the firepower if it had been needed.

After a much needed sleep of many blissful hours in the air conditioning of a Palawan hotel, Urban treated us to a tour of coast guard headquarters and a nearby fishing village on bamboo stilts over the shallow sea. His conversation was liberally interspersed with questions about New Zealand, immigration rules, job prospects and the like. We simply recommended he write to our embassy in Manila, a little sadly, offering 'to see what I could do to help' when I was home again. Later that day we flew out to Manila and a couple of nights wandering the establishments of MH Del Pilar in the company of another longtime mate, Kiwi Simon Halley, who was married into a local family and publishing an expatriate magazine online. Sadly, he too passed away a few years later. Finally though, we were onwards to New Zealand with the stuff of several magazine articles.

Back home I cast my bread upon the waters and a crust was picked up by my old employer, NZ Truth, my first customer for a Sulu Sea adventure report 'Down to a Secret Sea'.

Editor Hedley Mortlock, a taciturn fellow of formidable reputation and a 40 cigarettes a day habit even as workplace restrictions were coming in, assured me I was being paid 'more than any of the others' when he signed me up to an income that would boost the bank balance. I was back to recording the more salacious details of life, supported by a display and classified advertising section of the tabloid that kept the New Zealand sex industry boiling merrily along.

I continued weekend shifts at TV3 for a few months, before seven days proved onerous and I opted for a five day fairly casual approach. After many months the editorial subjects became a little tawdry and I was won't to remark to Sandy Macdonald who was a Truth sub that 'I was a long way from the Paris Peace Talks', as in my time with UPI.

CHAPTER TWENTY-TWO

AN EMBOSSED CARD arrived addressed to me by name, with the 'Master of the Royal Household' inviting moi to meet Her Majesty, Queen Elizabeth II and Prince Phillip at a cocktail reception at Auckland's Hilton Hotel, as the royal's were on yet another tour of the dominion. Of course the invitation was simply handed out by the Department of Internal Affairs and the clerk responsible had probably never read the content of Truth, which was well short of anything regal and had simply added it from an overall departmental media list. However, at the appointed hour, wearing an unaccustomed suit and tie, I presented myself at the Hilton Hotel and joined other media colleagues from stations high and low, in a line to shake hands with the regal couple, and then mixed and mingled.

In fact, Her Majesty proved very open company and while what goes on tour receptions is not for any media coverage, I can report in these lines a couple of decades plus and a new King later, that in our group of four journalists, the Queen had an animated discussion about racing and horses, observing that in New Zealand our jockeys went 'the wrong way round the track'. I was also sort of buttonholed by a pleasant, decidedly attractive and distinguished woman, apparently a lady in waiting who made sure I had a drink in my hand. It was most certainly a double, perhaps a triple, and she assured me that the Royal Household did not stint on such occasions. Standing about with my gammy leg is not something

I encourage and at one point I leant slightly against a wooden pillar beside a doorway. Almost disaster as it was apparently a temporary piece of decorative furniture with a large blue and white pottery thing on top. My move to lessen weight on my leg saw the pillar lean and the jar on top wobble alarmingly. Fortunately my gin and tonic lady put a hand on the other side of the wooden column and order was restored before disaster overtook the royal occasion. After she had chatted about what a fine visit she was having to New Zealand, she moved off towards a drinks waiter. Still slightly shaken by the near crashing disaster of the column I decided to slip away quietly, probably breaking protocol by leaving before Her Majesty. Well, this was my second media inspired Royal meeting and handshake, after all. I'm sure I could be forgiven such an indiscretion? On the way home I stopped at my regular watering hole to be told by colleagues I was "bloody late". I said I'd had had a previous appointment with the Queen. "Yeah, right, no bullshit. Have another drink mate."

My last 'story' on *Truth's* weekly look at the dark side of life was very far removed from high social engagements. It included a night assignment at a private fetish club party where a semi-naked idiot male was branded with a hot iron on his bum by a leather-clad equally strange female. Enough, I thought when the paper came out next day with a front page photo of the burning.

I decided on a complete change of scene. I had recently laid to rest my father who succumbed I believe to the final effects of high altitude wartime oxygen dosage, benzedrine boosts and being a prisoner of war in winter in Italy. Bronchitis never really went away, even after he gave up a heavy smoking habit. He had lived in a pensioner flat in Hastings in Hawke's Bay some 350km away. My elder sister Robin, an ex-nurse in the Royal New Zealand Airforce was married to her ex-RNZAF beau, Peter Wright, now a serving police officer. They also lived in Hastings and deciding it was time to catch up, I loaded up my car and headed south and west. I also took the opportunity for a lifestyle change. Apart from a sojourn on Great Barrier Island, I had lived in crowded environments from Canberra to London and Hong Kong and all points between. In Hastings, I looked for 'something in the country' and landed up on a rural farm 20km out of town, but with a nice rural pub not too far down the main road. To top things off, a seven-year-old beauty of a Border Collie working farm dog welcomed me to the farmhouse landlady Maureen's home with a strident bark, a cautious sniff and then full acceptance. We were joined at the hip from that day until he left me a little desolate 14 years of devoted companionship later, aged 21 years. His name was Sam and he had a vocabulary of some 100 words until deafness began to become evident in his last few years when hand signals and my facial expressions were quite sufficient.

The move heralded a stint of reasonably productive freelance work, aided immeasurably by an Internet modem connection that put me in instant touch with the world. I wrote for the *Sunday Star* in Auckland along with *Truth*, including a front page in the latter when I was handed the full set of keys to Mt Eden Prison in Auckland, courtesy of a patched local gang member who appeared to have an attack of conscience.

A good earner continued in Hong Kong, where Henry Parwani, now news director for a new multi-channel Star TV, which covered Asia was able to keep me busy. Oh the wonders of Internet and email. With Sam usually curled at my feet, the sun shining into the farmhouse with the swimming pool burbling outside the window, work was a breeze.

In addition to online tasks I was also contracted for several hours a day to the Hastings District Council, with an office off the mayor's suite, and charged with promoting the council's activities. One major event of this exercise was a huge bush and pastureland fire in an inland valley. A fleet of water-bombing helicopters and rural fire brigades with flames spreading rapidly in wind saw this reporter once again in the action. At one point flames jumped across a country gravel road over the top of our vehicle with a blast of heat that was more than a little terrifying as our vision was also obscured by smoke. However, in seconds we hit clear air, still on the road. I was able to brief the local media sufficiently afterwards to get a satisfying front page response for my employers.

CHAPTER TWENTY-THREE

ONE EXPECTS THINGS in life to change now and then and so it was when I called at my sister's home for a quick lunch one working day. I stepped through a gate at the side of her house carrying a hot roast chicken to share, with a cell phone in my other hand. Thus occupied I swung my hip to close the gate on its latch. But this involved an imbalance and trying to recover, my bad leg failed to relocate on the rough concrete path, staying in position while the body turned, resulting in a loud click as my leg suffered a spiral fracture.

It was an ambulance call and ultimately a three-week hospital stay. For the technically minded, it was a joint medial condyle fractured right tibia with a non-displaced fractured right shaft of tibia. An operation and five screws and a metal buttress plate sorted the main break and all was encased in a thigh-high plaster cast. It was all most inconvenient.

The accident kept me close to home and ended my council job due to travel restrictions with a couple of months on crutches.

However, I was soon kept busy on local research into an abiding mystery that appeared to me to be a great story, if it could be proven. This stemmed from a letter to the editor of a long defunct *Hawke's Bay Herald* edition of March 14th 1878. An old photocopy found its way into my hands and to explain further is to reproduce that document:

Sir, — Some time back, while visiting Te Aute

I was informed by an old bushman named Tommy O'Brian, who has long resided in the district, that there existed in the direction of Pokawa a number of limestone caves. To my mind there was something so straightforward and tangible in the tale told me that I determined to test the truthfulness of his statement, and with this object in view, Mr Owens and myself made arrangements with O'Brian to start on Friday morning last on a visit of inspection to the aforesaid caves.

At an early hour on that morning, the three of us started in the direction pointed out by O'Brian and after about three hours' rough travelling we found ourselves in a deep ravine surrounded by fantastically-shaped hills of limestone formation. The principal one of these hills we ascended, till about mid-way from the top. The travelling was bad in the extreme, in consequence of the density of the scrub and undergrowth, but O'Brian said, "You stand there, and I will soon show you cave number one." Owens and I willingly obeyed and had just commenced smoking when he shouted to us to come forward, as we were right at the mouth of the cave and true enough it was so, for, within a few paces of where we had stopped, and directly in front of us, was an opening into the hill guarded by gigantic trees. The opening I allude to is about 9 feet high and 6 feet wide, resembling a widely constructed Norman archway. This we entered, and by the aid of matches proceeded about 100 feet, and could have gone much further only we omitted to furnish ourselves with a supply of candles and lanterns, which we found would be essentially necessary for the investigation. However, for the distance we did go, we were amply repaid by seeing some of the most beautiful stalactites imaginable hanging from the roof and sides of the cave but our puny light scarcely afforded us an opportunity of appreciating their beauty and grandeur. So, after consulting, we determined to return to Te Aute and resume our search in the morning. That evening I procured a couple of lanterns and a supply of matches and candles together with 100 yards of strong line and were off by daybreak. Upon reaching our destination we made one end of the line fast to a tree growing in close proximity to the entrance of the cave. We then lighted a candle and proceeded cautiously in our work of exploration, noticing as we progressed that there were a number of lateral openings into the chamber we were traversing, and, as we advanced further onwards, we found a number of broken and unbroken pillars, rendering progress in some places both slow and difficult. This chamber, at about 100 yards from the entrance, is at least 40 feet wide and 20 feet high, forming from the roof to the top of the columns a symmetrically carved arch, from which, at this point, the stalactites are most profusely and singularly grouped, while, still more strange, there is a miniature lake surrounded by pale green shrubs, the whole appearing like a fairy bower overhung with crystal pendants. There are also in this sheet of water several inverted crystal cones, rising about 9ft out of the water. At this spot we lighted another lantern and as our line was at its full extent we deposited one lantern at the edge of the lake and proceeded forward, the scenery increasing in grandeur and beauty to such an extent that it baffles my feeble pen to do justice to it. It must be seen to be realised and appreciated. After we had proceeded about 50 yards from where we had deposited our lantern the chamber still increased in height and width, and on the right-hand side from the entrance we came upon a number of petrified bones, some of very large dimensions, as well as three human figures in a high state of preservation, apparently father, mother and child. I will not speculate as to how they came there, or what was the period of their coming. Near to this group, but on the opposite side of the cave there are rude sketches of warfare, and, from the countenances attempted to be depicted, I do not think they represent the Maori type of features — that is, of the existing race. From this point we retraced our steps, determined to further prosecute our search on Monday. In the meantime we have placed our discoveries in the hands of the Government, and if you think them worthy of publicity, I now place them at your disposal. — I am, Sir, Duncan Ogilvy Campbell, Te Aute, March 10th 1878.

I have no reason to assume any family connection

to the writer, but I was impressed with the detail which I decided had a strong element of truth therein. But where to start? I had built up something of an area knowledge, and there was Pokawa which lay north-west of the Te Aute Hotel, which was indeed my local watering hole. I had established some good local relationships with several farmers, workers and landowners among them. After several weeks of making enquiries, I seemed to have narrowed it down to an area of hills to the north-east of the pub bordering the wide Poukawa Valley that was mostly in the hands of the prominent Brownrigg agricultural empire.

Further talks however led to local doubts that I would get much further in my quest, with increasing indications from other farmers in the limestone hills north east of the valley that any caves in the area were more than likely closed with explosives to stop stock falling in, or perhaps children exploring. There was also the fact that in 1931 New Zealand's deadliest earthquake devastated Hawke's Bay killing at least 256 people. The earth moved in Pokawa where contemporary reports recorded hills moving and wire fences twanging like guitars. All the hills were now in private farm ownership and cleared of bush and trees mentioned as guarding the cave entrance. When it boiled down to it, I was still in a boot plaster cast and ill-equipped for any exploration, even if unlikely permission was granted. I did meet another local history buff who was determined to carry on the search. However, I have heard nothing since that time. The letter closing mentioned the writer had informed 'the Government' but there are no other available records to be found.

CHAPTER TWENTY-FOUR

As LIFE ALSO offers sometimes, when one door closes another opens and in my case it was an approach from the editor of a Waipukurau provincial newspaper the *Waipawa Mail*, seeking someone to record the history of a prominent local farmer, 90-year-old Tom Butler. It became the first in a series of projects that turned me to another professional bowstring, that of an author and historian.

With Sam in tow, I embarked on a series of interviews with Tom assisted by his daughter Josephine as we sourced family documents and indeed revisited Hawke's Bay rural locations where his forebears had played a major role in road construction and bridge building. At our first meeting Jo and I had a flash of recognition. It was soon evident that I was lying in a Hastings Hospital operating theatre having an x-ray probe of my leg injury site and she was a theatre nurse, huddled behind the portable x-ray unit to avoid unwanted regular radiation exposure. Small world strikes.

I had written Tom's life story up to the time of his marriage in the 1940s, when Jo was on the phone to say he had been rushed to hospital. I was able to visit him there on one occasion but he did not recover to return home.

We decided to publish his book, *Granddad's Room* complete with a selection of photographs where he had left his thoughts with me and it was successfully launched at a family function, selling out locally as an historical record of the district.

The book was opened with a foreword from a family friend, Sir Ian Lloyd McKay KNZM, a Judge of the Court of Appeal of New Zealand and member of the Privy Council, UK.

He wrote:

> Tom Butler has provided a fascinating account of his own family from the time his grandfather arrived from County Kerry in Ireland in 1875. The story covers the early settlement of an immigrant Irish family and their establishment in a new land by physical hard work. It tells of the early years of becoming established, of the milling of timber and transporting it by river, road and rail. Tom's grandfather then established a major contracting business, building roads, bridges and wooden viaducts then later settling on land in central Hawke's Bay and developing sheep and cattle farms. The story has much in common with those of other pioneering families. But by studying one such story in depth, one can best gain an understanding of what was achieved by the early pioneers and what has built the New Zealand we enjoy today. I would commend this book to all New Zealanders as portraying a vital part of our history. It is a history in which not only the descendants of the pioneers, but all our citizens can take pride.

Sir Ian set the seal for me in opening up an abiding interest in history and set me on a pathway to recording a wide knowledge of New Zealand rural history in a dozen mainly commissioned volumes over the next two decades, in addition to a resurgence in news gathering that completed a full circle back to my provisional newspaper roots of 1963.

But in closing Tom's account I must mention a snippet that to me highlighted the strangeness of the land those pioneers found themselves settling. Tom told of a family anecdote whereby his grandmother was given a 'bucket full of whitebait' by a farm worker. "But I will not feed worms to me family," she admonished the startled benefactor and she promptly poured the copious delicacy onto her vegetable patch Times have definitely changed since.

The fairly positive feedback from Tom Butler's book was soon followed by another approach to record a local family history and it was a red letter day too in establishing a long and valued close friendship. I still free-lanced, with in-house promotional television documentaries taking prominence. I worked with Hastings cameraman Simon Nixon, a stringer for TV3, on a series of projects for local businesses, vineyards, educational institutions and a farmer's market.

But on the book front, I was commissioned by a major Central Hawke's Bay farmer, Michael Hardy, to record his family history in the wider context of Hawke's Bay and New Zealand's development. It was a very rich mine to enter.

Michael and Jane Hardy farmed under the shadow of the Ruahine Ranges with extended family also farming in close proximity. From the day we met for an exchange of views and ideas on the proposed book, my companion Sam was part of the team with Mike and Jane's dog at the time, golden labrador Molly, providing canine companionship.

In common with many farming homesteads the Hardy home at his property, 'Lime Terrace', was a museum of documentation, photos and clippings tracing a myriad family events and accomplishments. I spent many days and nights on the property with most excellent hosts as I worked on our project, with the working and subsequent title *Footprints* (in the land).

I was beginning to establish something of a formula in preparing the local history accounts that I found of intense personal interest and liken this to constructing a house. First lay the foundation, erect a time-line, or 'scaffolding', and then add substance 'framing, cladding, then 'doors' and 'windows' and top it all off with a 'roof ' and paint and decoration, As a write through, before completion, add 'furnishing' to the creation.

With this in mind, *Footprints* began to take shape as a friendship grew apace. There were stories and anecdotes I learned that did not make it into the pages at first. But as we neared the completed manuscript, I thought about this and so then wrote:

> The sun sinks to the west of the rugged Ruahine range, throwing long shadows over Lime Terrace. A chilly southwesterly wind swirls around the house, and Michael throws more wood onto the crackling fireplace, which quickly warms the spacious lounge.

Glasses are topped up, glinting in the flickering flames as outside the dusk deepens over the gardens and tennis court. Molly the labrador lies contentedly at our feet and from the kitchen wafts the smell of herbs and the sizzling aroma of a leg of prime home-kill hogget.

We rest comfortably in armchairs and toast the close of a very pleasant day. On the coffee table lie more of the extensive collection of family photographs including an evocative shot of Lionel Eric, Michael's father, with horses on his Motunui Station among them. Michael says: "There are a million tales in every family that might not necessarily fit into the line of the story, so to speak. So how do we deal with that?"

Sitting here at the family hearth with the fire, the mellowing companionship and the hint of good food on the way, it suddenly strikes us both that we have just found the place for those anecdotes and fragments of family history that are extraneous to the main core of this account to can come to rest.

And so it was, in the closing 40 pages of *Footprints* we included rich snippets of stories, a portfolio of photos of family events, people and comprehensive family tree graphics, that give a huge sense of completeness to a unique narrative on New Zealand settlement and development.

I remember that final book launch with several hundred rural and urban guests at the settlement of Onga Onga, and I was called on to speak. I simply said that "in view of the hospitality being dispensed by our host on this memorable occasion in particular, I had best keep my counsel – simply because having enjoyed many a libation with Michael, I perhaps know more about him now than some people do – and I don't want to let anything slip in front of so many witnesses."

The dust-cover notes for *Footprints* demonstrates the extensive history it contains:

> Their surnames were Hardy, Gleason, Richie and Glenny linked now through marriage and seven generations to many other families, the length and breadth of the country. Families that took root here and whose descendants are woven into the social fabric of New Zealand today.
>
> From medical school in London when the scourge of typhoid was as prevalent as the common cold; from a potato patch in Ireland to the Ballarat goldfields; from a Scottish mansion and a whiskey distillery and from world renowned woollen mills in Scotland, they came by sail and steam to a new country on the far side of the world. Samuel Whittaker Hardy founded a Hawke's Bay farming family, Patrick 'Paddy' Gleason established hotels and businesses across the land, and David Ritchie farmed in Wanganui and Hawke's Bay. George Glenny also turned to the land.
>
> The descendants of these family patriarchs carved lives in many areas of endeavour.

Footprints is but a fragmentary reflection of 150 years of New Zealand's growth set down for generations yet to come. In this image, lies the substance of the people we are today.

CHAPTER TWENTY-FIVE

I WAS STILL involved in writing Footprints when I was sidetracked by something out of Ian Fleming's James Bond stories. I was approached by some Auckland friends who in turn had contacts with a group of ex-Special Air Service, soldiers who'd seen action in a number of world hot-spots and had retired from the military to form a security company. They called it Onix International and in SAS jargon trained at 'The Unit' an office and warehouse building in West Auckland. The company already had a contract to guard appearances of The America's Cup which was in New Zealand hands.

Two of their executive men had attended an industry conference in Australia and had been approached to effect the rescue of a millionaire Asian businessman being held for ransom in an Indonesian village. My friends had referred them to me as a possible writer to set down the rescue story for a book or even television exposure. Intrigued, I flew to Auckland and met Onix bosses, and over a number of meetings they told me how they managed to extract the businessman from his captors and get him back to New Zealand.

I have decided not to fully identify those involved in the mission in this book, as after 25 years I have no idea what they may have gone on to in their endeavours, although the company principals were a matter of record at the time of this event.

The rescue involved a team of eight former SAS men, a map of the village, and a reconnaissance visit to

Indonesia. Two men got to the window of an isolated village house and espied the captive businessman living in squalor and guarded by what appeared to be four members of a local gang.

The advance party retraced their steps for discussions at a Jakarta luxury hotel with Asian businessmen purporting to have access to millions of loose cash of the captive's fortune to back a rescue and offer a very substantial fee plus all expenses for service. The advance party flew back to Auckland and set up a mock target area in The Unit to practice the rescue mission.

Ready to go, off they flew again and bought two utility vehicles in Jakarta and travelled down to the target village some 200km away. I interviewed one of the participants immediately after the mission they dubbed 'Jet Li' for a proposed report that I have never used until now. It is evidence that the best-laid plan can go awry, in this case lack of attention to a train timetable almost ended the operation as a win was in sight. His account:

> As we turned onto the final road we could see the lights in the distance where the house was. The breathing was now coming faster as we hit the point of no return. We got Go! Go! Go! Nathan shot from the vehicle with myself right up his arse. As I entered the courtyard, I saw a shadow coming from his right with a weapon in his hand. I moved in to take the threat out and Nathan was there using his arm. He sent the guy flying against the wall about four feet into

the air. I moved to the next threat and pushed it aside. I heard the door being smashed open and bright light filled the courtyard from the room. More people moved into the yard yelling and shouting. The place seemed to be packed with people. I glanced towards my left and saw a figure running away. The man Nathan hit with his arm was still down and the lump of wood which I thought was a weapon was discarded to his side. Shane had his bundle (the captive businessman) held up high and came running towards me. I turned and followed back the way I came running in between the vehicles and in behind Bruce at the same time jumping into the back as Kenny was joining us. I was flying into the back as Bruce took off and Tony yelling go go go I saw people now running up to the front vehicle before they realised there was another behind it. We nearly ran a couple of them over as they were throwing rocks at it. And the captive was screaming "No,no.no.no" – a scream I will never forget. Kenny nearly hit me with his asp as he thought I was one of them coming back through the back door. I yelled at him it was me. The blood was pumping as the vehicles took off down the road. I was looking at the back watching for lights to follow but nothing was happening. We turned back onto the road and lights were flashing in front of us and our hearts sank thinking they had called the cops. Getting closer we realised it was a rail crossing barrier. It was down for a train. Nathan jumped out. Shane rushed across and they lifted the arm. We launched the vehicles across the track. I saw Nathan run across the track and as he did so the train went flying through with the horn blaring only missing him by centimetres. John was still going up the road with us yelling at him to stop as Shane raced past us in pursuit of him now nearly 250 metres further up the road.

I noticed to the side of the road locals sitting watching all this in total awe as we left them in our dust. The drive out to the main road was still hairy as the unknown was still in front of us. I kept looking back for the lights as we turned on to the main road. The comfort level still wasn't there, conversation was short and the blood was still racing. Everybody's still on edge we were nowhere yet home free.

Later the team established the actual 'snatch' had taken about 12 seconds – faster than it had ever been in practice. This segment of the rescue was never told as it seems there was no reward coming for Onix and it's believed the rescued businessman named as Johnson Cornelius Lo flew back to Asia from New Zealand to just disappear. Scant months later in December 2000, Onix International went into liquidation.

It was reported at that time a New Zealand Member of Parliament, one John Tamihere whose Waipareira Trust had a financial interest in Onix said he did not know the details of the company's closure but that the SAS veterans were 'the type of people that will reincarnate themselves somewhere else.'

CHAPTER TWENTY-SIX

THE 20TH CENTURY was about to roll over and the world's boffins dubbed it the millennium bug, and Y2K which they decided meant that the world would suffer a computer breakdown as the year 2000 dawned. When the personal computer took off in the 1980's programmes were written using a two-digit code for the year. Instead of a date reading for instance 1996, it read 96 because it saved data storage space.

As the year 2000 approached the whizz kids thought hell, the computers might not interpret 00 as 2000, but as 1900 and we will disappear backwards a century. Things would become difficult for banks, defence systems, airline bookings and flights and anything programmed on a calendar date would fly up the proverbial creek. It would be hard to fly anywhere in 1900 mate. Anyway the solution was not so hard. The date was simply expanded to a four-digit number and around the world the government and the computer industry worked to fix things. But the U.S. not all that surprisingly thought it detected Russian missile launches, but it was a long pre-planned exercise and nothing to do with computer bugs. Australia invested millions of dollars in preparing for a major event and all but shut down its embassy in Russia in case communications and transport went haywire. So in the end, casual acceptance of the Y2K threat overcame international hysteria and the world kept turning.

In my case however, the world actually stopped

on a personal level. An evening telephone call hit me between the eyes as my brother-in-law Peter informed me that my youngest sister, Jill, the mother of two young children had died suddenly from a brain embolism.

I was no stranger to bad news. In fact it was part of my profession, but nothing prepares you for the event when it is close to home. I managed to pull myself together and I drove to Auckland with my dog Sam in the passenger seat and with the sad and crowded funeral service over, my eulogy read, I stayed with a very long-time friend, Kathy, who I had known since my earliest days in Hong Kong. She had been a neighbour in our apartment complex, and moved to New Zealand with her family before we actually followed a year or so later. Kathy had worked in Special Branch for the Royal Hong Kong Police and was now single again and working as a media consultant.

Long conversations later, I was back in Hawke's Bay with unsettled thoughts. Before long, Sam and I were packed up and moving again, this time to a small village called Paparoa in Kaipara District north of Auckland.

Kathy had already moved there as had my old mate Sandy MacDonald so ready-made company was a bonus. After helping Kathy settle her relocated house in bushland adjacent to the village I soon found myself at a bachelor-friendly beach-house with a wide sundeck overlooking the broad expanse of the southern hemisphere's biggest natural harbour. My first undertaking was a new book as I seemed to have donned the mantle of author-historian. I had been put in touch with another prominent farmer, David Withers, whose 5,000 hectare property ranges over steep hill country in the hinterland of the Te Urewera National Park.

So once settled at Pahi, on the outskirts of Paparoa and a seaside village enclave of peace and quiet, geared up with a wireless internet, I found myself on the move once more deep into the back country to meet my new client. Sam found luxury accommodation in the meantime with my friend Kathy.

Dave's home, on park-like grounds in retirement from full-time work on his property, now run by family members, was on the banks of one of New Zealand's premier trout streams, the Ruakituri River that carves through the base of the valley of the same name. The title leapt out immediately as *Tales of the Ruakituri Valley*, and as my system has formed, I set this 'foundation' down after my week's stay with a great host who was to become a very good friend.

> Between the New Zealand North Island coastal provinces of Bay of Plenty and Hawke's Bay, steep rugged mountain ranges tower over precipitous valleys, pristine lakes nestle and rivers wind through narrow boulder strewn gorges.
>
> To the north and east the land steps grudgingly down through fertile farmland and forest blocks to the Pacific Ocean. To the west, it rolls more gently into the developed country of Waikato provincial dairy farms and to the south, into the

North Island's bleak volcanic plateau and its own guardian ranges.

This is the Urewera National Park encompassing some of New Zealand's most inaccessible country and formed around two million years ago when a geological cataclysm thrust the seabed into daylight. Mudstone, siltstone and sandstone in turn, some 15 million years old, has been layered in the detritus of pre-history, the fallout of the violent volcanic creation of New Zealand, carved now by weather, earthquake and time into a realm of mystery and beauty.

Fauna and flora have taken hold over the millennia and in the greening of summer, the air is redolent with the sounds and smells of uniquely New Zealand native forest. In winter, a frozen chill paints white the land, the mist rolls in and time stands still. It is a place both welcoming and unforgiving.

The focal point of this ancient scenic grandeur is a relatively recent addition, a lake. Around 100 years before the birth of Christ, an earthquake launched a landslide of sandstone, some eight kilometres long and four wide that fell across the Waikaretaheke River. The trapped waterway backed up behind the barrier and became Lake Waikaremoana.

Today it is the heart of the park 610 metres above sea level and holding nine cubic kilometres of water, constantly replenished by its parent waterway and fed too by an abundance of streams. Around the lake shore fingers of highland divide deep valley coves while on its southern shore the towering Panekiri Bluffs guard the country beyond. For an astonishing 2,127 square kilometres around the lake lies the fourth largest reserve in the country, and the greatest virgin indigenous forest in the North Island. Podocarp rainforest guards a myriad lesser species in the valleys rising up to 4,000 and 5,000 feet to mountain beech scattered around the tops. The park is home to an estimated 650 native species.

Among these are rimu and rata, totara, kahikatea, ponga and the ubiquitous manuka and a seemingly uncountable array of ground cover, ferns, grasses and mosses. The forest contains 35 native bird species. Tui, the cheeky kaka parrots, piwakawaka – the fantail, bellbirds, the sleek glossy kereru or wood pigeon and more rarely the New Zealand native thrush – pio pio, create a stunning daybreak chorus. The cries of the iconic kiwi, and the shy elusive morepork haunt the nights. The little seen whio Blue Mountain duck, graceful herons and gawky pukeko frequent the lakeside and waterways while the native falcon, karearea circles above.

Man is here too and the land is steeped in the legends of the Tuhoe Maori people who have coexisted for centuries in the rhythm of the magnificent, if uncompromising, heartland. The very name Te Urewera has its roots in the somewhat painful tale of an ancestral chief who died after rolling into a fire in his sleep. It translates as 'burnt penis'. Tuhoe claim their origins in the legendary marriage of the maiden of the mist, Hine-pokohu-rangi and the mountain Te Maunga. They are thus born of the supernatural – the Children of the Mist. Tuhoe warn the unwary visitor they are not alone as guardians of this land for Te Urewera is also the home of the patu parairehe, the fairy people. They may seldom be seen but be assured they are part of the forest.

Long of an independent nature the Tuhoe in the past threw up warrior leaders, the guerrilla leader Te Kooti and later the prophet Rua Kenana were both campaigners against the encroachment of European settlers in the 19th and early 20th centuries.

Today, their descendants are among the guardians of the parkland. Ancient Maori pathways are part of a network of tracks used by hunters and trappers. Dominating the eastern boundary of the park is the Huiarau Range and within its vast catchments there rises a river. It begins life modestly enough as a mountain stream that tumbles its merry way through gully and canyon before dropping through three levels over a spectacular 100 metre escarpment as the magnificent Waitangi falls. Below the falls, the river takes on a different character, reforming in greater strength, rolling down through rocky bush clad hills, curving its way past sandstone bluffs and sedimentary boulders out of the park environs to snake through valley pasturelands that bear its name – Ruakituri.

It is the life force of the Ruakituri Valley on the cusp of the Te Urewera National Park where magnificent sheep and cattle stations cleared from virgin bush towards the turn of the 19th century, bear witness to the endeavour of man. The river nurtures and ravages the land in turn, reflecting the wild weather swings that sweep the vast land of its birth.

It is a classic wilderness river and one of the best trout fisheries in the country with a deserved reputation as the source of the strongest, wildest rainbows and browns an angler may ever meet.

The Ruakituri River is also something much more. It is the giver and shaper of life, a link between two worlds, a conduit of history and the pathway to the future. Let us now embark upon a journey into this magnificent river valley and beyond.

I was to spend entertaining working weeks in numerous journeys to the valley to pore through documents and photographs and have long interviews with Dave covering a life of considerable achievement. From an apprenticeship as a high country shepherd, he went on to break in large farming properties and also serve as the leader of Land Search and Rescue in Te Urewera. He was also a leading horseman, and adds the letters QSM and JP to his name.

I travelled to the Ruakituri Valley as usual by road with Sam as a passenger curled in the backseat but waking up at full alert when gravel roads and stock aromas indicated the farm was close and often with good mate Adrian Blackburn, a handy sounding board and adviser on things literary. He was helpful too in drawing anecdotes from Dave's colourful past over an evening noggin or three. We launched *Tales of the Ruakituri Valley* in August 2006 to much district-wide fanfare at the local community hall, complete with venison barbecue, lots of home baking and liquid refreshment.

There were many trips afterwards because an enduring friendship that was a bonus.

CHAPTER TWENTY-SEVEN

THE JOURNEY OF discovery in the valley was also echoed on my new home turf in the Kaipara. One wet day, while still staying at Kathy's house, I was sorting through some family documents and came across my late mother's birth certificate, never sighted until that moment. I had always thought of her as born where my grandparents made their home in New Plymouth in my childhood. It was a shock to find I was now living about 100 metres as the crow flies from her birthplace – listed as the Schoolhouse, Schoolhouse Lane, Paparoa.

Investigation at the local library followed and with it a revelation that I had somehow completed a family circle. It was a moving experience after a big part of my life spent around cities and countries the world over. It transpired that my grandfather, A.K. Robertshaw, after service in the New Zealand Expeditionary Force in the First World War in France, found himself as headmaster of the Paparoa School, and his home was where my mother was born in 1922.

It was a discovery that would have sidebars in the near future as I became involved further in local history, starting with a visit to an iconic and internationally renowned local attraction, The Kauri Museum at Matakohe,

First opened as a wayside stop with a few local nicknacks and a produce store, the museum rapidly expanded over decades to showcase the rich history of the Kaipara with particular reference to the giant kauri tree that provided the lifeblood of early settlement My researches led to this summation:

In the mists of time, the Kaipara was a land of giant kauri trees, patrolled by giant moa, myriad lesser birds and with her seas and rivers abundant in fish – a place as near perhaps to paradise as ever existed.

Then came the Maori from out of the Pacific, an island people with a tradition of superlative navigation skills over the wide ocean tides and currents, cloud and winds that led them to Aotearoa, The Land of the Long White Cloud.

For centuries they made New Zealand their home. Then in the early 18th century came the tall ships of European explorers, followed swiftly by seal hunters, whalers, traders and an assortment of adventurers.

In the mid 1860's, came a wave of settlement by people seeking freedom from Europe's regimented class system and established social regimes. The Auckland Provincial Government offered assisted passages to immigrants from England and wider Europe and the northern Kaipara Harbour was selected for settlement. A man was offered 40 acres of land with a further 40 for his wife and 20 acres for each member of his family between the ages of five and 18.

In May 1862 the first party of what became known as Albertlanders set sail from the East India Docks in London. After some 100 days at sea, the immigrants were sent off to their place of settlement on the Kaipara. Maps dished out in London showed wide roads from Auckland clearly marked, but were in fact, nonexistent. Wagon wheels many immigrants had strapped to the ship rails were sold before they left the fledgling city and went by smaller watercraft up the east coast to the then coastal hamlet of Mangawhai, today a bustling town and seaside holiday destination.

From there it was a slow and arduous journey over bush-covered land to Kaiwaka and on by tidal waterway to Port Albert. In ensuing years, more migrants fanned out to claim land in and around the emerging settlements of Maungaturoto, Whakapirau, Pahi, Paparoa, Matakohe, and on to Ruawai and Dargaville.

An area of 70,000 acres of land was settled by the Albertlanders and Kaipara is today home to these towns with many surrounding farms still in the hands of those original families.

Port Albert, once seen as a provincial capital city to rival Auckland, still stands as a sleepy backwater off State Highway 16, with the town of Wellsford long replacing it, to then grow exponentially with the advent of railway and arterial roads.

The other main route to the Kaipara was by way of the west coast, via Helensville, then a timber milling town gorging on the huge Northland Kauri forest. This was the route of the Smith family, still resident in the Matakohe area today and with founding connections to the iconic Kauri Museum. The Smith matriarch was the first European woman to step ashore at Matakohe that afternoon in November 1862 and the family went into farming and kauri milling.

Land grants were made as surveyors completed their tasks, and many settlers lived in makeshift camps when they first landed ashore. As they moved onto their blocks, men supplemented their income until the land provided, by digging for kauri gum while the timber was harvested.

Gum along with fine timber was a valuable export, used in the manufacture of varnish and linoleum. They worked mainly in wetlands and swamps where once there were ancient kauri forests and around 450,000 tons, worth £25 million, were sent to England or North America between 1850 and 1950.

Huge tranches of timber first served as masts and spars for sailing ships of many nations, and later buildings rose in Sydney Town and as far away as Los Angeles from pit sawn and milled beams, joists and weatherboards.

Wise heads did not prevail until as late as 1970, when legislation halted the indiscriminate milling. A forest of more than a million hectares in the mid-1800s had by then been reduced by 90 percent. But even a million hectares may have been dwarfed by kauri's primeval forests, with ancient gum deposits found that were thrown up from the seabed, far from our shores.

All this is recorded and documented along with a

magnificent photographic collection much from the early glass plate wooden cameras some pioneers possessed. It was while I was browsing the collections that I was approached with the suggestion that I meet a local founding force of today's huge complex, a lady called Mavis Smith, even then approaching her centenary.

CHAPTER TWENTY-EIGHT

I visited Mavis Smith in her family home since her birth, Totara House, close to the museum itself and deeded to the institution in perpetuity. The family homestead was a collection in miniature and after a few visits and meetings I set up shop with my computer in the huge ballroom, with its full size billiard table acting as a sorting platform for documents. Above the table were the mounted heads and horns of a favoured bullock team from the kauri logging days, each with its name on a wooden mounting. I have always maintained that their constant glassy stare kept me up to the work in hand.

Mavis proved to have great recollection and a great wit and over some months and many cups of tea we together produced a book entitled most appropriately as *Child of the Kauri.*

My son Shaun was an accomplished graphic designer and oversaw the cover which was well received, with Mavis' face as a young girl apparently within a large piece of translucent kauri gum, together superimposed over a kauri forest and bush – the title in blue sky above.

Setting the foundations for the story began with Mavis opening thus:

> I was asked how long had I lived at Totara House? I said 95 years and I was born here.
>
> "Oh, how sad," was the reply. "I have moved about all my life. So I thought, have I had an interesting life?"

That made me think. I was born into a large and happy family, good parents, eight children, six brothers and two sisters. We were all so happy and we all helped each other throughout our lives and cared for and nursed each other until lives ended. And now I, Mavis, am the last.

So walk with me through these rooms of Totora House. And let me share with you some of the memories, the laughter and the joy, the happy times and the sad, the triumphs and the sorrows and the bubbling fun and humour this great house has seen through all the years.

Here's the kitchen, still with its wood-fired stove upon which water was boiled for a ton or two of tea leaves. Since the house was built in 1896 many other words of wisdom and otherwise have crossed the kauri kitchen table, the true family centre, where once my mother and father sat at each end and charted the course for my brothers and sister and I seated along the side.

Many other guests have also sat here, among them the occasional statesman. New Zealand's first native-born prime minister Joseph Gordon Coates, was a friend and neighbour. Large kauri cupboards have stored the wherewithal of the table, jams and preserves gathered from the home orchard and bottled every season. My father's hoard of tinned toheroas one time. There the hooks that held the home-cured hams and ducks and pheasants in the shooting season.

The kauri slab kitchen bench could have

been built yesterday, the result of long obeyed instructions that it never be left wet. Sand soap and fresh lemon juice have preserved it like new.

The huge kauri mantelpiece is a treasury of time and tradition, begun at the turn of last century, as seen in the names of family etched forever along the face of the shelf. This echo of yesterday is protected by the Historic Places Trust, as is the rest of the house. Come through with me now to the billiard room, dominated both by the billiard table itself and the kauri family table which seats 18 for dinner.

You see the Smith men were miller's of kauri at the turn of last century. And in 1895, a great log was bought out of the bush and from it seven table tops were cut, each 10 feet long, half as much wide and two inches thick. With one table going to each of my seven Smith uncles, the sons of my grandfather, Richard Christie, and grandmother Catherine.

All about the walls my grandparents, parents and siblings looked down to keep me company. My father George and my mother, Emily and her parents, George and Rachel Sheppard. They're framing this wonderful room with 75 magnificent, kauri wavy panels set in rewa rewa wood, the best of the best chosen and carefully put aside from the Smith mill. They were first French polished and now they glow from a century of tending with olive oil and a damp cloth.

This room opened after it was added to the house in 1919 with a grand ball. A lady of the day was performing an enthusiastic dance step and her heel damaged a panel. There has been no dancing in here ever since.

So let us step into grandma's room at the front of the house. This is always kept for visitors and is home to the Puriri Furniture, a chest of drawers, sideboard and Duchess Pair made from puriri wood, kauri and rewa rewa, bought in 1905 and cost 21 pounds 15 shillings and two pence plus two shillings and six pence in freight from Auckland.

We have been in and out of this room all our lives and the set is in the same condition as when it arrived, save a scratch that I inflicted with a hairpin when something provoked me as a small child.

The black Iron bedstead has been in this room always. The kauri wardrobe takes six men to move it. It was made just after the First World War when the builders here for the billiard room were called back to Dargaville to make coffins for the influenza epidemic. A man called Denis Campbell who was part Maori told my father, "I don't want to go, if I go back there, I'll know I'll die." So my father let him stay provided he built the wardrobe while he was here.

That kauri chest of drawers? One of the workmen was in trouble with the law and the police seized his tools in lieu of a fine. So Dad paid his fine and this chest was by way of a payback from the workman who built it in his spare time.

In the hallway is a lovely photograph of my mother and great grandmother on a bullock sled off to church in the mud. The bullock's are being driven by Alpha Matakohe Jervis, the first white child to be born in Matakohe. What a name. My father was the second white child born in the area, but he was only called George.

Oh, this house of a million memories. It echoes the years that have gone by with people shouting. "The insurance man is at the back door. The power board wants money. Dog dosing this afternoon. Have the bread and meat been delivered? Do you want the cattle trucks on Thursday? Bobby's got the tractor in the bog. Who will ring the hay-bailing man. I want the truck. Can you do a play for the drama school? When do we plant potatoes? We need flowers for the hall please....Such was the frenetic pace of life in my wonderful Totara House, once upon a time.

CHAPTER TWENTY-NINE

LOCAL NEWSPAPERS HAVE been likened to diaries for small towns and as the world has radically changed in how we communicate, rural community newspapers are having an upsurge.

The major metropolitans are facing a starve as is television, while the internet and social media takeover mass communication and with that an increasing advertising spend. But from time immemorial human interest has always been close to home. What is on offer in my town? Which tradesman can fix this problem on my house or my farm? What work opportunities are available? Is there a theatre group locally? What's the local sports team up too? The list of interests is endless and more and more the local newspaper fills a widespread community need.

I made casual contact with a small newspaper in Kaipara published by a company called North-West Multi Media when a friend suggested a local fishing contest might make an interesting item. Before much time went by I found myself back in my earliest reporting role being asked to keep an eye out for local events that might make news. Like Topsy, things grew and the bi-weekly tabloid offering became weekly, I became editor-at-large, the company expanded and was reinvented as Integrity Community Media and within a year or two, four major monthly regional farming titles were added. The company founder, Allan Mortensen, was a former printer by trade and had a simple philosophy – coverage of daily life happenings develop a sense of community through shared experience to mark the weddings, anniversaries, and obituaries, along with school events and successes. Local journalism in local community papers helps readers link neighbourhoods as well as civic and political engagement by covering news of local council decisions. On the provincial farming titles, Northland, Waikato, Taranaki and *Manawatu Farming Lifestyles*, the local regional pattern was supplemented by features that "looked over the farm gate" at the pursuits of the people on the land. There's something about print and photographs. They can be picked up again and passed on with information shared and discussed, instead of disappearing with the touch of a computer key. Having a local news medium helps create the identity of the place where you live.

Of course the lifeblood of any news operation is advertising and it sustains carefully targeted local newspapers to the extent that copies are delivered free. The advertising content is reaching a readership that is actively seeking information and answers. Businesses, small and large, need customers who are informed and particularly in spread-out rural areas, community press is an excellent business servant.

In my own case, regular employment all managed online and in comfort from my waterfront eyrie while my book assignments continued on occasion, was a new lease of life when many of my contemporaries were thinking of retirement.

I was looking at a story on a major community fund-raising campaign aimed at building a multi-million dollar dementia unit in a nearby town when my book with Mavis Smith produced an important dividend.

The Kauri Museum had become something of a haunt as I had been elected to the voluntary trust board that governed the 4,000-plus square metres of building enclosing myriad artefacts and information, including the largest collection of kauri gum on the planet, antique kauri furniture displayed in a two storey internal pioneer boarding house, as well as a huge collection of associated machinery and a working timber mill. There is a colonial dining room and if you look closely you will see the late Mavis Smith in effigy, as in the creation of exhibits many local faces were cast for posterity.

There is a huge collection of photographs on the museum walls and in the extensive archives and these became the catalyst for a major coffee-table book and collection that I was asked to undertake.

When the vast kauri forests of Northland and the Coromandel Peninsula were being plundered for the prized timber early last century, a young man of 22 years named Tudor Washington Collins took his camera to work in the bush camps of the time. When he died in 1970, his bequeathed collection of more than 2,000 photos found a permanent home at the museum. So began a long investigation into his world as I set out to record an extraordinary contribution to the nation's history. It was also something of a team effort with the museum staff ever helpful in locating relevant material and records from which I could develop the written text to 100 black and white plates that were digitised for the final manuscript.

After many months, the landscape edition of *Kauri Cameraman – Tudor Washington Collins 1898-1970*, was designed and published by my son Shaun's company, with this introduction:

Among his many occupations, Tudor Collins was a sailor, a bushman, a businessman, entrepreneur, traveller, farmer, and when time permitted, bon vivant. Above all he was an extraordinarily gifted photographer, who single-handedly captured the essence of the history of New Zealand as he strode the earth in his 72 years span. Along the way he flew in the Southern Cross with Sir Charles Kingsford Smith, walked the ruins of the Napier earthquake, served in the army and the Royal New Zealand Navy in two world wars, travelled the Pacific with Lord Mountbatten, conversed with Her Majesty Queen Elizabeth and fished in the Bay of Islands with the novelist Zane Grey.

The extent of his photographic impact is such that a total accounting may never be fully made. However, one perception that dominates the ledger is his love of the tall trees, the kauri. At The Kauri Museum, the Tudor Collins wing houses some of his bequeathed collection of kauri industry photographs. There are the deep hidden depths of the kauri forests, the fit hard main of the bush, the people of the gum fields, the bush camps, the mighty dams, the horses and bullocks and above all, the magnificent trees that have all but vanished from the landscape.

It is a journey into yesteryear through the lens of a master photographer, who once said, "I've never used a light meter in my life, judging an exposure if it was sunny by the feel of the sun on the back of my neck, and if it was dull by the light on my eyes, I wouldn't say I always got it perfect, but I usually wasn't far out.

But while taking photographs, Tudor was also a working man and his experience in a dangerous world made his success with a camera all the more remarkable. His notes from that time recorded several close calls:

> It was at No Gum Camp that I took to climbing for the gum lodged in the branches of the trees by means of spiked clogs, and steel hooks. This occurred on Sundays, the only days for washing and doing odd jobs. The gum fetched five pounds a sack from the buyer and the extra money was secured at great peril.

He set off with his hooks and climbing spikes and usually a rope.

> On one occasion I had no rope. So after climbing the tree and collecting some gum, I had to back pedal down, lowering myself on the hooks, a much more difficult undertaking than going up.
>
> When I was about 25 feet from the ground, I was horrified to notice that one of the hooks was spreading out. There was nothing I could do except shin down as quickly as possible.

But I had not lowered myself more than another five feet when the hook broke right off. I could get no grip on the smooth trunk of the tree, which had a girth of 12 feet. By getting a slight hold with my arms I managed to stay upright and slid down at a terrific speed. I fell backwards on the sloping ground and injured my spine on a root. I lay there for two hours or more and then managed to crawl home to the shanty only about 200 yards away. I hoped to keep my escapade secret, but my brother Jim found out what had happened. He said I was too good to get killed that way. And he took away my climbing boots.

Kauri Cameraman was launched in style at The Kauri Museum with some 300 guests present, including, I was thrilled to see, my friends Michael and Jane Hardy who travelled up from Central Hawke's Bay for the occasion. In fact it transpired that the working mill at the museum came from the back of their Hawke's Bay property.

Mind you, such things are not always plain sailing. Two hours before the event, with all preparations complete, we had no books! Frantic phone calls found they were on the final road to the museum. With literally minutes to spare, a completely overloaded utility vehicle backed up to a side door with the tray hard on the rear springs from the weight of 1,000 copies. It transpired that the driver had travelled from Wellington overnight, after the book publisher wrongly addressed the shipment, not to Kaipara, in

Northland, but to 'Northland' a suburb of Wellington – 640km away.

Of the consignment 500 copies were numbered in a Limited Edition, with gold title script and a series of extra pages and photos of Tudor in other walks of his life. These were half gone by the time a few of us close to the project and some friends and supporters had, that evening, opened another bottle of celebratory wine.

CHAPTER THIRTY

THE MUSEUM FRATERNITY in New Zealand is close knit in a nation of just six million people and it was not long at all before I was approached again, this time by the iconic Albertland Heritage Museum in the town of Wellsford mentioned earlier in these pages.

Peter Marsh from the museum was the grandson of Harold Marsh, 1876-1948, a farmer and above all a photographer who more than equalled the groundbreaking record of Tudor Collins and the kauri by documenting the lives of his peers in the early years of last century.

Peter was overseeing a huge collection including glass plate photos being digitised and our connection became cemented with news of the success of my Kauri Museum project. A history then of the Albertland settlement in more detail is important to background the production of a second 'coffee-table' look at a major New Zealand story and photographic record.

In August 1861, there existed a National Association for Promoting Special Settlements in New Zealand with two events driving such emigration – the American Civil War had diverted the stream and the Bi-Centenary of the expulsion of Nonconforming ministers from the Church of England. The latter led to plans for a Nonconformist Special Settlement party for New Zealand. The name chosen for the new colony was 'Albert Land' following the death on December 14th 1861 of Prince Albert, husband of Queen Victoria. In preparation, in 1862 a survey party set out in a whale boat from Auckland.

A settler had to pay his own way and to live on his property for five years before he was granted the freehold.

The first two ships, *Matilda Wattenbach* and the *Hanover*, set sail on May 29th 1862, with the *William Miles* leaving on July 29th 1862. Sailing ships of that time did not make landfall en route and passengers expected to be at sea for 100 days or more. It was not always plain sailing either. The *Matilda Wattenbach* made the passage in 93 days despite losing her main and mizzen top masts in a storm 300 miles north of the Cape of Good Hope.

Auckland was the arrival port and of course contagious disease was a risk on long ocean voyages. The *Tyburnia* was quarantined off Rangitoto island with smallpox on board, although only one passenger died. Aboard the *Annie Wilson* on a calm day in the tropics, some drunk crew members mutinied. The captain and officers managed to regain control.

Finally about 3,000 settlers were to arrive here but for many, Auckland was the end of the journey. They heard about primitive conditions in the North and so settled down and were absorbed into the business, trade, and commerce of the young Auckland.

A ballot had been made prior to arrival to determine ownership of land covered in bush. Maps were scarce and the settlers had some difficulty finding their allotted acres. Tents were a luxury of the fortunate. A tarpaulin stretched over a frame of poles was more than many had.

Bush shanties were built with split slab walls and a solid thatch of nikau fronds for the roof. Later, pit sawn timber was used for weatherboards, with split kauri shingles on the roof.

By the spring of 1863, progress had been made with 80 families numbering some 220 souls living on their new land to the north and east of the Kaipara Harbour. Paddocks had been cleared, in some cases fenced, and sown in grass.

A notable recollection of the museum today is that local paramount Maori chiefs, Paikea and Arama Karaka, welcomed the Albertlanders. Paikea said "You are my Pakeha, and I and my tribe will be ever ready to protect you with our bodies. You have much to teach us, and you may learn many things from us that will be useful to you. May we be brothers forever. That is the wish of Paikea."

Armed thus with a glimpse of history I set about researching the massive 7,500 plate collection that features families, events, people, boats, weddings, farming, fishing – a real potpourri glimpse of life in Albertland and beyond in the early 1900s. My task was to select a short list of 200 black and white now digitised treasures from Harold's lens. It was a time consuming but fascinating task.

With Peter and his family members and staff, I explored the comprehensive displays and also a vast genealogical base to put together a text to compliment the chosen photo plates and the result was 150 pages of *Images from Albertland* which was launched including a 'silver edition' at a town function which included valued support from my good friend and neighbour, poet extraordinaire, Sam Hunt.

Publication actually coincided with the 150th anniversary of the Albertland settlement and this fact led to another remembered string in my bow, video production. With the knowledge gained in the book exercise I was asked to put together a commemorative record on CD. This involved tracing the Albertlanders journey from landing in Auckland through to Port Albert and staging stops in between. I had to make a number of stand up dissertations to narrate the story links and that was fine on day one. A late night dinner catchup with old friends in the city saw me a little bleary-eyed for my first on-camera sting next morning but fortunately it was not obvious in the finished product, which pretty much sold out at anniversary festive functions in the district.

CHAPTER THIRTY-ONE

WHILE CONTINUING MY Editor-at-Large role, I was able to move about pretty freely and this has been the miracle of computers and the Internet. I was online reading some British publications and came across the by-line of a journalist that I knew to be the sister of my friend from UPI days, Mike Poole. It was the work of moments to relay my contact details through the British newspaper to its lady writer, who in turn alerted Mike.

With contact re-established for some years, the time came for a visit to my old stamping ground and I flew off to Europe with travelling companion Adrian Blackburn again. Travel in fact had become a breeze with the advances in aviation and the long and somewhat exhausting journeys of my earlier travels had been accelerated to the point where we flew Qatar airways from Auckland to Doha in one hop of 18 hours in a Boeing 777 and after 90 minutes in transit another six quick hours in an Airbus A380 to Paris. Business class in my case added the luxury of comfort and sleep.

We had booked a self-drive hire car from Charles de Gaulle airport and planned a series of articles in France for my newspapers that included tracking down the Somme grave-sites of several local area servicemen from the 1914-18 war. We drove out of Paris planning a breakfast stop en route northwards but we had made a bad miscalculation. It was July 14th, the French National holiday celebrating the revolution, Bastille

217

Day, and the country was basically shut down outside the busy airport. We didn't find sustenance until midday at a small family restaurant open to travellers. But it was a delicious lunch of fresh fish and garden vegetables. Refortified, it was on to the Somme and the rather bleak but immaculately manicured cemeteries that France supervises with ongoing care and attention. In the New Zealand cemetery a greater proportion of headstones, row upon row, simply bear the legend 'A New Zealand Soldier of the Great War' but the names of all the fallen are listed from regimental records on a nearby memorial wall and I was able to identify my local men and place a poppy beside their names for a photo.

We also spent a day at the medieval walled village of le Quesnoy, liberated by New Zealanders from the Germans in that war and the site of a monument and museum commemorating the event and a close relationship between the town and New Zealand. In fact as we had some lunch in a town square bistro a local man, perhaps over-hearing our conversation and accents, simply walked up unannounced shook each of us heartily by the hand, before continuing on his way. However, while we managed to get photographs, including a group of French school children on a fact finding outing at a high stone wall climbed by Kiwi soldiers on wooden ladders, with a memorial plaque engraved, it was still part of France's Bastille observance. This curtailed our proposed inquiries at the town information office. The visit still provided stories for the local kiwi paper mills as we headed our car to Calais and a ferry across the English Channel.

This was a bit of an eye opener. As we enjoyed an evening beer at a bar in Calais we couldn't miss the appearance as dusk fell of dozens of people gathered in alleys, doorways and street corners in the CBD area. These were refugees on their desperate journey from the Middle East and North Africa, ever hopeful of finding a way to Britain and a new life. Presumably people smuggling deals were in the making in darkened doorways and alleys as we made our careful way through the few streets to our hotel for the night. At a restaurant for dinner downstairs, we met our waiter resplendent in an All Blacks copy rugby shirt. We were happy to adorn it with a silver fern souvenir pin that I had come equipped with as a cheap thank-you gift on our travels. That prompted a round of liqueurs.

The next morning, passports and tickets in hand we had no access problems and a pleasant ferry crossing to Dover to set off to drive to Mike's home in Devon. This journey was notable for an incident as we followed our GPS voice companion and took a shortcut into the main street of a small town to find it lined with flag-waving and cheering locals as we drove past them. There was a placard reading 'Welcome the Olympics' and it dawned upon us, we had strayed ahead of the torch-bearing event heading for the games venue in London. Our shiny new Peugeot had French hire-car number plates suggesting we were something new and worth cheering on. Shades of my London red carpet theatre welcome of many years past. Commenting on it, Blackburn suggested I not make a habit of such things.

We arrived at Mike's home in the historic village of Bere Ferrers, on the banks of the Tamar River near Plymouth, with Cornwall across the waterway, to a warm welcome from Mike and his lovely wife Chrissy and wonderful rooms on the upper floor of an imposing old mini-mansion. There ensued several days of social pleasantry and many reminiscences of Fleet Street, now of course history as all the newspapers headquartered there in our day had long since been relocated to the wilds of suburban Wapping. There were visits to the historic local pub where even Sir Francis Drake's crew might have once supped ale adding to local lore. But Bere Ferrers has a New Zealand-focussed, but tragic history, that made good material for a piece I wrote for *New Zealand Memories,* a quality magazine periodical that is a must for students of the past.

At a number of places in Bere Ferrers are memorial's to 10 New Zealand soldiers who were killed in a railway tragedy at the village station in 1917. Apart from signage at the station there is a memorial inside the local 13th century church and a monument in the neighbouring village of Bere Alston. The soldiers were killed and two injured after the troopships *Ulimaroa* and *Norman* had just arrived at Plymouth from New Zealand. The men boarded a train at the docks headed for Sling Camp on Salisbury Plain when disaster struck. Their troop train was pulled up at Bere Ferrers station where the line ahead was a single track. The troop train had to wait until it could proceed but the soldiers on board apparently thought they had arrived at a planned meal stop at

Exeter. The train was long and several carriages were short of the platform. With Exeter then as the first stop and according to instructions, two men from each compartment were to get out and draw rations from the brake van. When the train pulled up and almost before it had come to a stop a number of men from the rear coaches jumped on to the track seeking food. The soldiers were raw, sick, weary and bloody hungry as they'd not had anything since embarking at 6am and it was now almost 4pm.

> They were mowed down by the London to Plymouth express as it roared through the station on schedule and carnage followed. The express driver slammed on brakes and the express pulled up about a quarter of mile later. One of the survivors later described the moment of impact:
>
> We never thought of an express travelling 40 miles an hour. They don't travel at that rate in New Zealand. It was a wonder more of us were not killed. I saw the coat-tails of the man in front of me fly up, and I picked his body up afterwards some yards down the line.

Other soldiers were also ordered to pick up their dead comrades from the track and place their bodies in the goods shed at the station which was turned into a temporary mortuary.

The dead were buried in a military cemetery in nearby Plymouth. Each year since that dreadful day the people of the area hold a remembrance service, always attended by New Zealand visitors and VIPs.

After a lovely visit and local exploration, Blackburn drove off to visit family staying on holiday elsewhere in Britain and I joined Mike and Chrissy who were headed off for a French holiday on an overnight ferry and a very long drive across France to be dropped off to stay with a very good friend from my Hong Kong days in Dordogne. There is much to be remembered over fine French dining in towns like Sarlat and Montignac, and historic St. Amand de Coly and accommodation in a grand chateau restored from the ruins of a 500-year-old nunnery that is the story for another time. However, France also provided more material for the farming papers back home, including an encounter with a fox trapped in a special cage. With the species unknown in New Zealand, where chickens free range with abandon, it was an intriguing farm yard. A wire cage with a trigger floor dropping a mesh gate was set up near a recently fox-raided chook house and the bait was two plump fowl, a rooster and a hen, caged in an inner compartment with food and water in the mid section. Blackburn had rejoined the 'tour' from UK and our hosts had left us 'in charge' of the chateau and 50 acres of walnut plantation while they in turn went on holiday for a couple of weeks.

We checked the trap each day, with nothing but slightly restless chooks. But then after about a week, there it was. The door had dropped into place from the animal's paw pressure. On instructions left us, we notified a neighbouring walnut grower and later that day heard a muted rifle shot from the cage area. In point of fact, I have always felt since writing an article for New Zealand rural consumption, that I might have just let the nice furry alert wee fox escape before sealing its fate. But more dead poultry would probably have led to a major guilt trip.

CHAPTER THIRTY-TWO

AFTER I RETURNED to New Zealand, fate did its thing again and I walked out of a medical consultation and examination diagnosed with bowel cancer.

It happened thus. On the Kaipara Harbour's great expanse, fishing was a pleasant pastime and good too for the table. I was at the wheel of a 30 foot launch when I hit a near whirlpool eddy around a headland point as the tide ran, violently rolling the boat and damaging my ribs in an impact with a fire-extinguisher fixed in the wheelhouse. Still far from our landing, I scoffed a rather generous handful of aspirin to cope with the pain on the home run. The next morning, blood in the bathroom sent me to the doctor and then on to the emergency department at the hospital in the major town of Whangarei. After admission, and many blood tests and scans, the cancer diagnosis was given an 80 to 20 per cent positive prognosis. The oncologist put down my lack of any early symptoms to "you are lucky you cracked your ribs. The aspirin thins the blood and triggered a bleed in the tumour that you might never have felt in pain terms until it would have been too bloody late." Suffice to say five weeks of extended radiation, a five hour 'complex' surgery with two weeks in hospital followed by seventh months of oral chemo was a major hassle with much out-patient monitoring and a stoma bag for 12 months. Finally this was followed after a year by more surgery for a resection reversal. All now a bit of a blur. I believe – a bit like my poliomyelitis recollection, the mind has a way of folding less pleasant memories into some corner to keep it subdued. But I took another year to properly recover. I still had my editorial role to fulfil but I also decided to apply myself to a long held objective of completing a novel as I convalesced.

I had had the title of a piece of fiction, based a little on fact, since my time visiting the Philippines on both assignments and just plain R and R. I always recalled a trip in a taxi on a Christmas morning circa mid-1980s. I was with mates in Manila while working in TV and with the Philippines capital only an hour or so from Hong Kong by Cathay Pacific Tri-Star, I had volunteered to cover a Christmas Day shift to let family staff take time out. Thus with Kai Tak airport just down the road from the TVB studios I flew back, worked a shift, and flew back to Manila in time for happy hour.

En route to the airport, stopped at a red light, a street waif of about six years old tapped on my taxi window. It was half open in the heat and I looked into his grey-green eyes. "Sir. Me no Christmas," he said quite clearly. He was obviously of mixed race in a part of town where many tourists from around the world formed local liaisons and returned to their home countries oblivious of the consequences for young bar girls with too little education on the facts of life. Anyway, I carried small denomination notes in my safari jacket pocket for airport tips and such. I thrust a couple of peso notes into his hands just as the cab-driver got the green light. I looked out the rear window as we drove away to see the lad accosted by older children. No doubt his money would have gone into the street gang coffers. But I have always wondered about the kid's background and what might have been his future, and this became the stuff of a novel I penned in succeeding months, entitled initially as *Me, No Christmas*. However it was eventually, with much fictional and imaginative addition, published worldwide in the UK as *City of Storms*, and still lists on Amazon in print and eBook form.

I was also still fascinated by local history and as I have indicated at home just metres above the Kaipara Harbour waters, I was in a good place to do a suggested potted history of the wider district which attracted some 100,000 visitors a year when the local and world economies were in alignment. The harbour of course is a jewel in the national geographic crown as I wrote in a tourist-oriented contribution called *Kaipara Timelines*, featuring selected historic photographs from the local museums, some already reproduced in my earlier coffee table volumes.

Kaipara Harbour is one of the largest in the world covering 947 square kilometres at high tide and surrounded by an 800 kilometre shoreline. It extends for some 60 kilometres from north to south and has catchments feeding five rivers that emerge from drowned valleys, earning them the name of salt rivers, and over a hundred streams.

Sheltered waters belie a fiery past though, for this was once part of a giant Kaipara volcano that erupted some 20 million years ago. There are numerous studies that indicate pyroclastic flows of volcanic ash and gas swept eastwards from the offshore volcano. Near Tinopai a visitor can still see geological layers indicating ash and giant kauri trees reduced to timeworn petrified stumps.

Today, on average, tides rise and fall 2.10 metres Spring tidal flows reach 9km/h in the entrance channel and move 1,990 million cubic metres per tidal movement or 7,960 million cubic metres daily.

The harbour heads are dangerous – waves from the Tasman Sea break over large sandbanks about five metres below the surface, two to five kilometres from the shore, an area called The Graveyard and responsible for more shipwrecks than any other place in New Zealand. For this reason, the Kaipara is rarely used today for shipping.

The harbour is a huge migratory bird habitat of international significance. Forty–two coastal species are known, and up to 50,000 birds are common. Rare species such as the godwit use the harbour for feeding during summer before returning to the northern hemisphere to breed. Species also include fernbird, fairy tern, crake, Australasian bittern, banded rail, grey-faced petrels, banded and NZ dotterels, South Island pied oyster-catcher, pied stilt, and wrybill.

Land habitats adjacent to the harbour support some rare botanical species, including native orchids, the king fern, and the endangered kaka beak. The edible fern (para) was good to eat (kai) – creating the Maori name Kaipara.

Despite the perilous bar at the harbour entrance, the

Kaipara became a busy timber port from the 1860s, shipping thousands of tonnes of kauri timber and gum.

The Northern Wairoa is the main river feeding the Kaipara from the north and the town of Dargaville was established on the timber and gum trade 30 kilometres upstream. In the hey-day of the kauri trade, huge rafts of logs were brought down the river to mills about the shores of the harbour. By 1907, production had peaked, after which a steady decline set in, with only minor amounts being cut in the next 50 years.

During the 1950s and early '60s, the supply of logs from private lands almost ceased. By 1973, government policy finally ended all felling of kauri. Fortunately, massive replanting projects have come into play since – but it will be many lifetimes before these trees gain historic stature.

After 1920 the gum and timber industries dwindled and farming took over.

From the harbour waters still come abundant fish, and the area is the major snapper breeding ground for the waters of the west coast. Mullet, flounder, sole, kahawai, trevally, gurnard, rays and sharks also abound. Oysters and scallops are also on the seafood menu, today farmed where once they could be freely gathered in the wild.

CHAPTER THIRTY-THREE

THE SLIM VOLUME on art paper was a quality printing that took the reader through the Kaipara district and was welcomed by the district museums and local tourist venues. One of those was the Dargaville Museum and a visit there found me admiring the adjacent Kaipara Vintage Machinery Club, a large complex over several acres encompassing a collection of machinery and implements from the establishing years of the county's agricultural development.

Serendipity strikes again and Kaipara Lifestyler publisher, Allan Mortensen was walking in town when he ran into a local identity, one Bruce Galloway, a prominent retired farmer and a founder of the vintage machinery project, who mentioned that he had a story he'd been writing, but that he needed "a bit of help." Mortensen mentioned my name to Bruce and pretty soon cups of tea and scones were on the table at his home and some writing plans laid.

Over some six months, a substantial volume emerged that I edited and polished with Bruce, as well as triaging a vast photographic collection. Bruce had penned the hard yards by hand in his retirement years, with a hard copy typed by a family member. I chose the role as 'project director' to bring the original manuscript to a professional level and arrange for design and publishing. The book 'blurb' for what we titled *The Flying Farmer*, by Wildside Publishing encapsulates 200 A4 portrait pages and copious photos.

A New Zealand farmer's memoir like nothing you've ever read before. a fair dinkum Kiwi bloke who broke in farms the hard way, had heaps of misadventures and close calls, including crashing his Cessna 182 aeroplane and just surviving to tell the tale.

There is more than enough in this autobiography of a hard working adventurous cockie to keep everyone who's fascinated with the history of rural New Zealand, up all hours of the night. Bruce was born and bred a country boy and the youngest of four children In 1942. His parents owned a 530 acre sheep and beef farm south of Danniverk in Hawke's Bay at a little place called Waiaruhe. In those days it was home to a school and a dairy factory. Both have since gone.

During his life, Bruce owned 11 different farms and many houses. He married Edna in 1964 and they were together until she passed away in 2013. He now enjoys life with his second wife, Juliet, children, grandchildren, and great grandchildren. This is a story of a genuine family man, with a great sense of humour, adventure, and love for family and friends."

In fact Bruce became a full-time farmer at the age of 16, after growing up when things were so remote from modern times as to bear recounting here.

> Mum was a great gardener, not flowers, just vegetables. She used to say you could not eat flowers. She had a large commercial garden and

supplied a local shop in Dannevirke. She also milked cows, cut manuka and raised a family. Mum was also a great cook and used only a coal range. There was no fridge and all the washing was done by hand and water heated by a wood-fired copper.

When a mutton was killed, there was only a short window to eat it before it went off. Mum used to preserve eggs in a four gallon tin and they would last up to a year. Some vegetables were preserved in stone crocks.

Dad used to cure his own bacon and it would hang up in the back porch for months. Mum would chop some off and cook it. The bacon used to turn green, but was still ok to eat. There was always plenty of bottled fruit. Mum would always have plenty of baking in tins, so we never went hungry.

Mum and Dad used to tell us stories of what it was like starting off in 1932. A track had to be cut through the manuka to get to the only building on the farm, a one room bach. Clearing the manuka was the top priority with both of them cutting it with hand slashers.

Dad put a tin shelter up over a bath and the water was heated over a fire. Mum did cooking and baking on an outside fireplace in camp ovens. The water was carried up from the stream in four gallon kerosene tins. They also told us about having to take the house cows down to the neighbour's bull to get them in calf. Mum and Dad lived like this for many months. We never had a flush toilet, just a long drop that had to be cleared of large two or three inch long weta at night before sitting down.

As kids one of our pastimes was to harness a horse up, drag a couple of big wooden dray wheels up to the top of a big hill, then let them go. Those things would travel at colossal speed, sometimes jumping 15 feet off the ground, and end up in the swamp. They occasionally changed direction and took out a fence or two. Once at the bottom, we would ride down and start all over again.

Summertime was spent swimming in the Raparapawai river or the old farm dams. Ice cream was something we did not get a lot of. We used to put some cochineal, mixed with milk, in a billy and hang it on the clothesline on a frosty night. It turned out more like ice, but it was good.

Bruce has long since lived a full and productive life although hampered in later years after crashing his Cessna in severe wind turbulence on a hillside farm paddock in 1980. The impact severed his right foot by 95 per cent and led to three months in hospital. But in retirement he was unstoppable and as the founding member of what is now Kaipara Heritage Machinery Inc.

Bruce Galloway explains:

It all happened like this.
Over the months of June and July in 2001 I put several ads in the local Dargaville newspaper

inviting anyone interested in a local vintage machinery club to a meeting to be held at our farm at Te Kopuru on the 30th of August 2001. I received a number of replies and as a result six men came to the first meeting, along with seven apologies.

For nine months, we had our monthly club meetings at our farmhouse. I was really lucky. My late wife Edna was just as keen on the vintage club as I was and always put on a good supper afterwards. Some of the guys used to say they only came to the meetings for the feed! We liked to think we were a friendly family club and this spirit has been key to the whole time the club has been going.

It wasn't too long before word spread in the wider community and donated machinery and equipment was coming in. It was the obvious question of where do we put the gear?

In the interim, we decided to get out there and show off some of our tractors in particular. And the Dargaville Christmas parade was a very successful day with our first ever display attempt. It was great advertising for our club at the end of the 2001 year and in March 2002 it was all go. In the many years from this small beginning, we now have a membership of around 100. Our club buildings, some plant and funds are now valued at more than $2.5 million.

His continuing energy and drive has created an exhibition which led to his fellow members seeking a permanent record. Thus I found myself putting the keyboard to work once more. my second book *Vintage Memories* drew upon a wide selection of contributions from many members, past and present, of the society fully illustrated with a photographic record of characters and property milestones.

CHAPTER THIRTY-FOUR

OVER MANY YEARS I have sat with Dave Withers over a red wine and a venison casserole in his 'place in paradise' beside the roaring Ruatukri River and reminisced about some missing colour transparencies that he took as a young shepherd on the huge Ngamatea Station in the central North Island.

I had seen some of them when I wrote his *Tales* book and in fact used two of them as illustrations. But I remembered there were a lot more and where they had got to was a mystery. I was determined to locate them because modern digital technology meant they could be hugely enhanced to high-resolution colour plates depicting a history of New Zealand farming that would otherwise be lost. Dave hit his rural network and after several years in fact, the original transparencies still in their plastic boxes were located. They had been cared for by the family of one of Dave's shepherding day colleagues who had passed away.

These were valuable cargo and with the assistance of Adrian Blackburn, interrupting his hopeful pursuit of another mistress, the slides were brought to Auckland and processed by a tech expert into digital images. These were sent off on Dropbox into the ether and picked up by my son Shaun at his studio in Dunedin at the other end of the country. My text followed and all was formatted into *Ngamatea On Golden Hills*, 100 colour plates and accompanying text beautifully presented by JOP Print in Whangarei. It records life circa 1960 on the high country station, before the days of quad bikes and helicopters, when horses, dogs, a rifle and bush huts with a long drop were the tools of a shepherd's toil. Dave recalls:

> This was real outstanding country and I actually lied about my age when I applied for the job, as I had been told that Lawrence Roberts, the owner, wouldn't take anyone under 21. Of course, when my 21st birthday actually came around, word leaked out, and I was caught out. Mr. Roberts just grinned and shook my hand.
>
> A welcome gift from my mother arrived at the station. It was a Braun Praktica camera that arrived on horseback and then remained permanently at hand in my saddlebags. It had a light meter and I pretty much became self taught in its operation. The following pages were made possible by this wonderful gift.
>
> Boy, that central North Island high country could be cold. I remember line huts where rainwater ran cold and deep across the dirt floor. Weather so cold we were constantly shivering and snowed into huts, so bored we would reread the descriptions on cereal packets, sauce bottles, and the like.
>
> But it was not always winter and high summer in the rolling hills was a joy. In the aptly named Golden Hills, the musterer's hut was a frequent home.
>
> "Despite their youth, most of the musterers were engaged on long and hard working days,

with daily survival an integral part of their efforts," says Dave.

We would move big lumps of sheep, sometimes 2,000 strong, with just two men and a few dogs, not always successfully in the early days of my tenure, and come rain or shine.

But it was not all work and no play. There was great adventure as well. Deer hunting was a popular diversion and I shot my share of good stags. By the same token I remember once coming over a hill and there was a big 14 pointer just looking at me. He was in velvet, and his antlers appeared to be wavering in the wind. There was a picture to behold and I kept my rifle lowered. The moment was far too magic to spoil and he soon sauntered away free."

That was not the case on another occasion though, with a very different outcome. One day Dave Wedd and I were working when we heard stags down the bottom of a gully, so after we finished for the day, we went out to the deer. We blew a couple over and it was just on dark and Dave and I had got a bit carried away with these stags, chasing them around and the night was plugging in on us. It's blooming cold, you're up 4,000 feet or so. Trudging towards where we believed the hut to be we were in drizzle and fog and it became pretty dangerous. We thought we've got to make a decision or we can keep stumbling around in the dark. We were all on rock, no vegetation, just rock. We were only in Swandries, long pants, boots, balaclava covers.

Luckily a bit of tobacco but wet matches couldn't even light a smoke.

This was getting serious. We could tip over the edge we thought so we've got to make a camp here. So we found a little rock ledge to camp on, no cover. But for safety we had to stay put, huddled together in the cold. Nothing to eat. Tobacco chewed and spat out. We kept on this rock ledge until the early hours of the morning. And we had our hands up inside those Balaclava covers and then breathing on them. And every now and then we'd do a few gymnastic sort of exercises to stop us freezing up altogether.

Daylight and we're out of there over the ridge, down the face and into the hut. Not so far away after all.

The boys were all there and what did they say? "Oh you buggers have come back? We've already divided all your gear up – the dogs and your saddles and horses." They were relieved to see us come back but they were not going to admit that.

Dave and I were blue all day. The cold was deep into us. The boys gave us a hot breakfast but we couldn't get warm. Great mates, good camaraderie, but gee, it was close. If it had snowed we would have been in dire straits.

CHAPTER THIRTY-FIVE

It was while I was engaged in early talks on Flying Farmer that an event occurred that signalled a worldwide radical change in the whole business of news gathering and dissemination, the "profession" or more correctly "the craft" of journalism, the Fourth Estate.

This was the Covid pandemic that hit the world as I knew it in February 2020. I had a break from work and writing with another visit to the chateau in France, where in fact I had been granted 'Paul's Room' an en suite in a second story 'tower' and getting away from the southern winter for pool-side barbecues and fine French food in the surrounding region was very rewarding.

But as spring arrived I was back home for summer that was a little short lived as first news of the Corona virus leaked from China in January 2020 and suddenly the world was reeling.

In retrospect the New Zealand response to this event can best be described as draconian and in years since, the term 'long Covid' has been bandied about with various levels of authority but more about that in a media concept a little later. For the record the disease in New Zealand led to a reported 3,000 deaths and my home in Kaipara in Northland was affected along with the nation and the wider world as the government closed the country's borders and imposed lockdown restrictions. Those were unique in light of the country's geographic isolation that effectively stranded thousands of Kiwis in places around the world who had to ballot for the right to come home to limited quarantine prison camps, a measure which is now regarded as a major breach of human rights and may still be subject to legal redress.

Travel was restricted in regional community lockdowns, businesses were shut down, schools closed, mass compulsory vaccinations were organised, special electronic proof of the jab issued, face masks were mandatory and if there was ever a war footing, New Zealand was on one. Life as we knew it was radically changed.

On the work front, one edition of our weekly newspaper was cancelled before someone woke up to the fact that it was a vital community link in a pandemic health situation. I found myself as a working journo able to move about reasonably freely, but with the tools of my trade already well established in working from home for many years, my life pretty much continued as normal. For many thousands of fellow Kiwis, suddenly trying to work from isolation, let alone manage family life in lockdown, was a step too far.

I simply continued my lifestyle pursuit of a daily happy-hour catch-up with my neighbours in our self-declared 'bubble' and kept the paper informed of regional developments by Internet contact with the health authorities.

But for most New Zealanders the restrictions were a nightmare. Family disruptions by decree will have lifetime effects. Government borrowed billions to ease the pain of lost jobs but the simple fact that vaccine mandates meant those opposed to the needle lost jobs and livelihoods is an ongoing and acrimonious debate. It sparked mid-pandemic with a storm at the Wellington Parliament as some 3,000 demonstrators gathered to protest the government's action.

This turned into a three week occupation and something of a circus too. Protesters blockaded streets with their vehicles and set up camps on the government grounds and surrounding areas and disrupted lives in the capital in general. There was a Kafkaesque reaction from the seat of power though with the then Speaker of the House Trevor Mallard choosing to turn on the lawn sprinklers to soak the protest camp and anyone in range, kids included and also blast the gathering with loud repetitive music over hastily erected amplifiers. The cops called to control the crowds were not impressed by what one senor cop described as "the actions of clown." When Mallard was later sent off as our ambassador to Ireland, there were a number of "Irish" jokes that still remain in circulation. However, the protest was forcibly ended by police in scenes of confrontation, arson and physical violence that shocked the nation on prime time television. There were certainly no concessions from the government although after the furore died down I noticed an official plea for volunteers to help clean up the mess left behind.

Closer to home, restrictions finally disappeared in August 2023 and while it is still around and pretty much relegated to a bad cold or flu the pandemic has had a major impact on life around the world with a particular negative aspect on business and the media.

For an example, a thriving luncheon business has gone broke because former customers in nearby high rise offices are now efficiently working from home that was initially enforced by COVID restrictions. Corporations have found themselves saving millions in rent and power budgets. Empty offices mean no lunchtime customers seeking sustenance. This supply business fail is a problem in cities the world over. The new pattern of remote work is evident when you turn on the TV news to see an interview conducted on Skype or another application. Suddenly the cost of running vehicles and camera crews can be reduced. But with the rising use of social media as I refer to in the opening pages of this missive are one of the true enemies of today's media outlets.

Remote work and new communication tools are affecting many other sectors such as health care and education, but the news media has been hardest hit by both the Internet and social media as advertising spending goes swinging off to digital streaming. Telecommunication with little or no direct human contact has become a normal way of life. The impact though has been devastating as shown in New Zealand where my old employer, TV3, renamed at some time as News Hub, and owned by a US media conglomerate, stopped transmission with the loss of hundreds of jobs and little prospect of new openings in an embattled medium facing a rapid decline in advertising support.

News Hub was shut down by multi-billion dollar Warner Bros. whose Discovery Asia Pacific president James Gibbons, said the decision came after cascading negative events.

> "We are acutely aware of our position in the local media landscape and what this means for our people, and for the country as a whole," he said. "The impacts of the economic downturn have been severe, and the bounce-back has not materialised as expected. Advertising revenue in New Zealand has disappeared far more quickly than our ability to manage this reduction, and to drive the business to profitability. All over the world, media companies face very tough circumstances", Mr Gibbons continued. "Subsidising losses for ongoing years indefinitely is not sustainable."

The finances of traditional TV media speak volumes as in 2022, Warner Bros. Discovery lost $35 million before tax. The studio owns HBO, streaming service Max, Warner Bros Entertainment, CNN and Discovery and has in the climate of the Hub shutdown had debt of $US44 billion, with massive competition from Netflix and Disney streaming services.

As a journalist of many years, I have had a hand in training many young aspirants to the craft, and a recurring piece of advice has been "go for the quote. You are reporting what people say and not interpreting what they say. So if you provide an accurate quote you are doing the job right."

So abiding by my own rule, Warner's Glen Kyne says:

> "Free-to-air and news are expensive businesses

to run. Put simply, the economic headwinds mean the returns are not there. Even if Facebook and Google were to disappear, I don't think journalism could come back. It's not just that there's no money due to lack of ads; it's more that there's no time for readers to engage with it even if it's free. I myself read 'news' of one kind or another almost all day every day, but I'm hard put to sit down and engage with somebody else's gatekeeper package of news. And I am a journalist myself, so if I don't read it, who would? It's an absence, but it's also like thinking that a country needs a president instead of just some weird sort-of celebrity who makes stuff up on social media. Well, sure, a 'country' needs that, but it needs a functional first estate in the way it needs a functional fourth estate."

I wonder what new forms of social organisation can emerge from the rubble of all this. Fake news is also too common and a measure of its destructive power can be measured by the US Congress, where so-called lawmakers are on record. Apart from Republicans misguidedly enamoured with Donald Trump, some have actually acted on totally fabricated information about the Ukraine conflict that's proven to come from the Kremlin to make their decisions on funding and other aid.

There is a new journalist's 'round' in the media business, such as it is, with the creation of a byline identifying a 'Social Media Reporter' whose occupation is simply to troll through endless pages of X or Tik Tok or Facebook or some other un-named service that I am totally unaware of because I simply refuse to participate in the genre. Of course there might be a limit to the new reporting as demonstrated by the demise of the iconic *News of the World in Britain* after the scandal broke of journalists monitoring private cell phone calls, including those of royalty who probably still have shudders at indignity suffered.

Old habits die hard and I will certainly be left behind in the long run. I say this simply because social media has become the medium of choice for everyone from the British royal family to the heads of government, industry and business the world over. The days when a messenger would deliver a typed statement to the nearest news outlet are long gone. If you want to say something of note you do what those from the White House to the Élysée and Buckingham Palaces do and stick it up in X or whatever takes your fancy. We don't need news outlets to disseminate information and this adds to my earlier observation that what news outlets still exist are using social media instead of qualified staff to implore anyone on the scene of an event to act for them.

It gets worse though because at Facebook, someone called Mark Zuckerberg is on record of planning a 'news feed' that is a personal newspaper for every person in the world.

I certainly admit that I can't remember buying an actual printed newspaper. almost forever, because if I wasn't in the news business anyway, I always check on-line bona fide mastheads as a daily ritual but am often disappointed in the quantity of social media generated content. When I strike a paywall, the applicable headline gives me enough info to surf and find a version for free. So I certainly understand the changing face of the 4th estate be it newsprint or television. Radio will always find a place simply because it is aural and available in any mode, like the death of the Pope when I was 30,000 feet over Texas one time.

For social media companies the vast numbers that click into them create the actual content for free. It's a licence to print money. But that demise in traditional media is having dire consequences around the globe. There have been pundits claiming government support must step in but I believe most card carrying journalists would object loudly as what craft independence remains would disappear in a cloud of political party suspicion.

Here in New Zealand a technical institute 'Centre for Journalism, Media and Democracy' conducted a survey that says that general trust in the news and news brands is continuing to erode and finds news avoidance in New Zealand is at a high level, when compared internationally. 'People are avoiding the news because they find it depressing, negative, and it is increasing their anxiety. Many people also find news repetitive, boring and overly dramatic,' said the report.

Another major dampening of enthusiasm for the craft has come from the United Nations with Secretary-General António Guterres citing disinformation, hate speech and deadly attacks against journalists as threatening freedom of the press worldwide. His comments came on so-called World Press Freedom Day, that apparently is marked each year on May 3rd. Certainly news to this journalist of more than six decades in the business.

> "Freedom of the press is the foundation of democracy and justice. It gives all of us the facts we need to shape opinions and speak truth to power. But in every corner of the world, freedom of the press is under attack," Mr. Guterres said.

I would rephrase that by saying the craft itself, the 4th Estate, is also in dire straits.
New York Times, publisher A.G. Sulzberger:

> Without journalists to provide news and information that people can depend on, I fear we will continue to see the unravelling of civic bonds, the erosion of democratic norms, and the weakening of the trust in institutions and in each other that is so essential to the global order.

He said the same technology that allowed journalists to reach people everywhere, also forced many thousands of newspapers to close and digital outlets that emerged were unable to fill the void, particularly in providing critical local and investigative reporting.

In Paris there has been a conference to discuss draft global guidelines for regulating digital platforms with a call to uphold the right to seek and receive information in the face of rising disinformation online.

But to my mind, that horse has already long bolted and altruistic action plans are like some climate change dreams. As Kiwi government minister Shane Jones says "it's kissing unicorns."

As I near the close of this saga in 2024, the latest news from one of the most trusted and admired correspondents of the BBC I met briefly as a young man at a pub near Bush House, not far away from UPI's London operation off Fleet Street, is somewhat prophetic.

At the time of writing he's the corporation's International Editor Jeremy Bowen, predicting the Israel-Gaza debacle to spill over into a wider Middle East conflict. I suggest its a matter of if not when if you look at the situation since 1948. Add that to the tension in the South China Sea, the choice of Trump, by so many American voters, simply the passage of time means the world news story will never be exhausted. Just perhaps its veracity as the noise of today's choice of communication deafens us all.

But I must also point out that the prevalent distortion of facts bought on in recent years is in fact not all that new. There was a young reporter in Brussels in the early 1990s who excelled in stretching the facts to make a story.

He was famous for fabricating a report under a British press headline that ran 'Italy fails to measure up on condoms', with the story reading 'Brussels bureaucrats have shown their legendary attention to detail by rejecting new specifications for condom dimensions', despite demands from the Italian rubber industry for a smaller minimum width. The reporter told his readers that 'Italian egos are smarting' and quoted an official spokesperson Willy Hélin.

However, Mr Helin has gone on record as telling Britain's *Guardian* newspaper he was exasperated by the "load of bullshit" that was written. "He was the paramount of exaggeration and distortion and lies. He was a clown – a successful clown." He was describing Boris Johnson who went on to become British Prime Minister. The rest of course, is Brexit History.

Maybe the more things change, the more they might stay the same but the continuing multiplication of communication channels in this 21st century is out of our control. Today it is simply Vale! The Fourth Estate.

APPENDIX

Published Works:
Granddad's Room.
 Avlona Press. ISBN 0-47309522-X
 History of the Butler family and patriarch Tom covering Central Hawke's Bay farming and transport infrastructure. Illustrated.

Footprints.
 Press Gang. ISBN 0-476-01188-4
 Comprehensive Hardy, Gleeson, Ritchie and Glenny inter-connected families based on a farming, business, commercial and national hotel empire. Illustrated.

Tales of the Ruakituri Valley.
 Te Rau Press. ISBN 8-0-473-12095-5
 The history of a high country farm and the story of Te Urewera "Between the central North Island provinces of Bay of Plenty and Hawke's Bay. Steep, rugged mountain ranges tower over precipitous valleys, pristine lakes nestle and rivers wind through narrow precipitous gorges."

Child of the Kauri.
 Configuration Design. ISBN 0-473-11264-7
 The history of the pioneer Smith family through the eyes of Mavis Smith, including early kauri industry and The Kauri Museum development. Reprinting 2024.

Kauri Cameraman.
 Tudor Washington Collins Configuration design Ltd. ISBN 978-0-473-12340-6

Text and b/w plates for The Kauri Museum included a numbered Limited Edition.

Images from Albertland.
Echo Publishing Ltd. ISBN 978-0-473-18548-0
A history of Albertland through the lens of early photographer Harold Marsh. b/w plates.

City of Storms.
Oxford eBooks. UK. ISBN 978-1-908387-99-8
A novel set in the Philippines, fact-based fiction. Also available as an eBook on Amazon.

Kaipara Timelines.
Self published. JOP Print.
A booklet covering a brief history of Kaipara's settlement with b/w plates.

The Flying Farmer.
As producer/editor.
Wild Side Publishing. ISBN 978-0-473-51687-1
The comprehensive farming history (11 New Zealand farms) of Dargaville Vintage museum founder, Bruce Galloway. Illustrated.

Vintage Memories.
Producer/editor.
Wildside Publishing.
The history of the Dargaville Heritage Society and museum. Illustrated.

Ngamatea, On Golden Hills.
JOP Print. ISBN 978-0-473-68884-2
The story of a young high country shepherd and the colour transparencies he took in 1960s enhanced and digitised as colour plates after going 'missing' for six decades.

www.ingramcontent.com/pod-product-compliance
Lightning Source LLC
Chambersburg PA
CBHW030035100526
44590CB00011B/209